BWELL FOREVER

Celebrating Well-Being, Forever

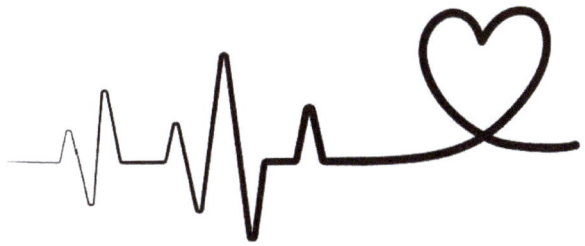

DR. BEENA WALAWALKAR

BLUEROSE PUBLISHERS
India | U.K.

Copyright © Dr.Beena Walawalkar 2024

All rights reserved by author. No part of this publication may be reproduced, stored in a retrieval system or transmitted in any form or by any means, electronic, mechanical, photocopying, recording or otherwise, without the prior permission of the author. Although every precaution has been taken to verify the accuracy of the information contained herein, the publisher assumes no responsibility for any errors or omissions. No liability is assumed for damages that may result from the use of information contained within.
BlueRose Publishers takes no responsibility for any damages, losses, or liabilities that may arise from the use or misuse of the information, products, or services provided in this publication.

For permissions requests or inquiries regarding this publication,
please contact:

BLUEROSE PUBLISHERS
www.BlueRoseONE.com
info@bluerosepublishers.com
+91 8882 898 898
+4407342408967

ISBN: 978-93-6261-587-9

Cover design: Shivam
Typesetting: Namrata Saini

First Edition: December 2024

Disclaimer

Before you start your fitness adventure, talk to your doctor, especially if you've never exercised before or haven't been active in the last year. If you encounter discomfort or pain while exercising, stop right away and seek medical attention.

While every effort has been made to verify the authenticity of the information contained in this book, it is not intended as a substitute for medical consultation with medical practitioner The publisher and author are in no way liable for the use of information contained in the book

All of the content in this book, including text, pictures, photographs, third-party information, workouts, diets, and psychological advice, is provided only for informative and instructional reasons.

This book is offered with the understanding that it will not be leased, resold, hired out, or distributed in any manner. The publisher's express authorization is required for any reproduction, in whole or in part.

Contents

Introduction 1

Chapter 1: Dr. Beena's Perception of TYBM and EPS 6

Chapter 2: The Secret of Fitness from Childhood to Old Age 13

Chapter 3: Exercise Happiness Paradox...27

Chapter 4: Health span vs Life span and Exercise Science 36

Chapter 5: Fitness Foundation 59

Chapter 6: Joint Health Is the Only Way to be............................... 99

Chapter 7: Yoga –Way to Go... 121

Chapter 8: The Best Style Is Ergonomics......................................139

Chapter 9: Just Let Your Stress Fly Away......................................159

Chapter 10: Healthy is New Happy 170

Chapter 11: Body Composition 179

Chapter 12: Fat but Fit Paradox..196

Chapter 13: Fitness on the Go..199

Chapter 14: Posture: The New Beauty Standard 205

Chapter 15: Putting It All Together 217

Introduction

"The doctor of the future will give little medicine but will interest his patients in the care of the human frame, Diet, and in the cause and Prevention of disease."
-Thomas A. Edison

Health is beauty, and fitness is its key.

The future of medicine faces the challenge of "Life Span Vs. Health Span." While life span refers to the total number of years we live, health span pertains to the duration that we remain healthy, disease-free, or maintain full functionality. Lifestyle habits make it easier to achieve this delicate balance, with diet, exercise, and self-care.

TYBM: Train Your Body and Mind and EPS (Extra Potential Stimulation)

Combining the intrinsic power of our body and mind with *EPS (extra potential stimulation)*, enables us to go beyond conventional boundaries and find innovative solutions to life's challenges. This book is based on these two mantras, TYBM and EPS, with the aim of empowering you to enhance your health span from childhood to adulthood.

A Short Note from the Author

I am a Doctor of Physiotherapy with a PhD in Physical Medicine and Rehabilitation from the USA. My journey with this book began during my early years as a physiotherapy specialist in a government hospital in the early '90s. During this period, I was a fresh graduate eager to absorb knowledge and provide the best possible care to my patients. It was a time when residual polio cases still lingered, predominantly in rural Maharashtra. These children, often from economically disadvantaged backgrounds, would travel great distances to seek treatment, with their parents displaying unwavering determination to help them regain their mobility.

In the depths of these rural communities, I observed how minimal education could inspire creative solutions. Parents devised creative methods, like seating their non-walking children in plastic buckets with holes for legs or repurposing everyday items into rudimentary wheelchairs. This experience has profoundly influenced my approach to healthcare throughout my career. Over the years, I have observed that when patients and their families are highly motivated and harness their bodies and minds, utilizing extra potential stimulation, remarkable recoveries become possible.

In the latter part of my career, I expanded my practice as a Rehabilitation Medicine Specialist, delving into the treatment of various conditions, from pain management to musculoskeletal disorders, trauma, neurological issues, cardiac rehabilitation, sports-related injuries, women's health, pediatric rehabilitation, and geriatric rehabilitation. In all my areas of practice, I have consistently observed that patients recover more fully and rapidly when they go above and beyond their normal capabilities.

Just as a woman transforms into a mother upon the birth of her child, a doctor is often deemed a great healer when patients achieve extraordinary recoveries. I firmly believe that if patients and caregivers are highly motivated and leverage their bodies and minds, along with Extra Potential Stimulation, remarkable accomplishments can be achieved in the realm of health and wellness.

I sincerely hope that you will find the contents of this book both insightful and enriching. It is my aspiration that the knowledge shared within these pages will provide you with fresh perspectives on life, offering new meanings to your everyday experiences and contributing to a graceful and enjoyable journey through the ageing process. I would like to express my gratitude for choosing to invest in this book. While exercise advice can be found freely from various sources, your decision to acquire this book suggests a commitment to comprehensive well-being and a desire to gain valuable insights. This book aims to offer not only a fresh outlook on life but also provides simple yet highly practical exercise recommendations that can enhance your journey through the various stages of life.

Why use this book?

"TYBM and EPS are the Mantra."

This book revolves around the art and science of physical and mental fitness by embracing the principles of TYBM and EPS. It is designed to empower you to overcome the conventional effects of aging on the body and mind and extend your health span.

When we are born, we face two choices: to die young or to continue aging gracefully. Nobody wishes to shorten their life, so our only inevitable path is to age gracefully. This book provides guidance on how to navigate the common and natural aging processes affecting the body and mind and how to make this journey joyful and fulfilling. It does not offer miraculous weight loss formulas, spot-reduction techniques, or mental tranquility shortcuts. Instead, it offers scientifically sound advice that anyone can follow.

In this book, I have attempted to accomplish two vital objectives:

Explain that fitness is more than just one element like walking, dieting, or practicing yoga. It is a holistic approach that encompasses five pillars of fitness.

Emphasize that every individual has unique needs, both physically and emotionally, which may evolve over their lifetime as they face different challenges. This book will help you identify and address those unique needs.

This book is founded on scientific research and my personal professional experiences over 25 years of patient care. In today's world, there is an abundance of information on health and fitness, often conflicting and overwhelming. I have filtered out the hype from genuine knowledge to present you with the fundamental principles of fitness that you can trust and follow.

How do we use this book?

The book is structured around **five major pillars:**

1. Fitness
2. Nutrition
3. Rest
4. Attitude

5. *Mental Health*

Understanding these pillars is crucial for making informed decisions about your health and well-being. The first chapter delves into TYBM (Train Your Body and Mind) and EPS (Extra Potential Stimulation). To achieve TYBM, you must set goals and maintain healthy relationships, while EPS requires you to unlock your full potential and think creatively to maintain your health.

Most chapters include Quick Facts, DIYs (Do It Yourself), and tables for easy reference. Sample charts and exercise routines are also provided in some chapters focusing on the six joints (shoulder, elbow, wrist, hip, knee and ankle) and spine which can be followed in the guidance of a professional.

I deliberately focus on both physical and mental health, as I believe they are intertwined. By gaining a deeper understanding of your body and mind, you will be better equipped to discern between myths and genuine information, resist the allure of the latest fitness trends, and embark on a journey of lasting well-being.

In this modern era, our focus should be on a healthy life span, and this book will be your guide to achieving it

CHAPTER 1

Dr. Beena's Perception of TYBM and EPS

The greatest thing in life is to keep your mind young.

I've often heard people saying that they are aged by numbers by young by their heart and I can't stress enough this line. One can still live young in his 80s if he knows the key. Yes, he can, and the key is to train your body and mind (TYBM) by tapping into your extra potential stimulation (EPS). The major concern of the chapter is to make people aware of what they can do with their full potential and trained body and mind.

EPS is essentially an individual's ability to go beyond and think out of the box to get a solution in whatever situation life puts him into. A person at 80 can smile back at his loss while a 30-year-old might feel sad or disheartened. Keeping your health in check is a key factor of living a happy and healthy life. There come times when you get to prioritize between your health or wealth. You must be thinking that you would've chosen health because why not. But this is not the real thing, we run after wealth our entire life thinking that we will take rest when we get enough money in hand. And when our health decides to leave our side, we don't even get time to use that money.

In my medical career of more than 20 years, I've seen people lying on death beds and making confessions about not taking out time for health or prioritizing it when needed. I agree that money is important but health is a priority. People need to understand this to the deepest that your wealth is all worthless if it can't keep your health. I am going to share two stories of those people who had lots of money but what happened when they were on their death bed.

Mr Nair and His Regret to Learn from

It was a lovely Monday morning. I had my complete workout which included stretching, strengthening, mobility, and cardio followed by a full healthy breakfast. So I was in a really cool and happy mood when I reached my clinic. As mentioned in my introduction I am a physio rehabilitation consultant working in the international market for more than 20 years. Show my clinics are always filled with people who require rehabilitation after sports injuries, trauma or chronic pain management, cardiac rehabilitation, and so on.

When I enter the clinic I had a walk-in patient in a wheelchair, a 70-year-old man, Mr Nair. I was surprised to see him in a wheelchair, quite both deteriorated in health and tired. He was a knee placement patient and I had treated him with post-surgical rehabilitation a few years back. He was back to normal life on his on-field after complete surgical rehabilitation. During the treatment session, I realized he was not taking care of his health and was not listening to his family and particularly his wife. He had presented himself as the real miser, a person who holds health and spends as little money as possible.

During the entire treatment, he used to talk about his life and his goals. He was a very wealthy person and worked really hard to earn this money throughout his life. His only goal in life was to earn money but not to spend it on anything. His wife was so unhappy as he has not allowed her to spend money on anything she likes in her entire life. Working hard and collecting the money for the bank, was his motto. I told him once "Mr Nair you are no less than a poor man in life but a rich person by Bank. Money has to be used in the proper time and manner, especially when you are young."

To this question, he used to say that he will enjoy and make full use of money when he will really retire. I asked him when he was going to get a tire to which I replied that the day he said all to work would be considered his retirement day. By then he had not travelled anywhere nor visited the best restaurants for good food with the family. He was waiting for his entire life to retire and enjoy the money. Now after 10 years, he was in front of me. I asked him what made him come here and he said "I am here to give the message for you to convey to all your patients, give meet or people you have in your life."

Apparently, his wife had died four years ago and he was in the terminal stage of lung cancer. On meeting he said "talk to you asked me to enjoy my life in the present. Enjoy my life and I can. But I never really bothered and look at me now I have only a few months left to live and my wife has already died. My kids have grown and left the home to start their own life. I lived my entire life to have money that has no value right now. Just a piece of paper dying in the bank. Neither my dead wife can enjoy it, nor me, as I will die soon and my kids might not need that money. I lived my life without any goal as a poor person and dying as a rich man is the biggest regret of my life. Please convey my message to people to keep goals in life and cherish your health and the people you love. Enjoy life to the fullest. Enjoy your life and present."

"Money Can't Buy Happiness," Says Mr Jame

Not just Mr Nair, but now Mr Jame shared something that made me realize how important it is to prioritize our health, relationships and goals in life.

One lovely morning, Mr Jame was having his coffee on his balcony overlooking the seafront with his dog named boxer, sitting next to him. Boxer was his only friend as he was a general manager of a deputy company so never got to live in any place for more than 3 years. That morning Mr Jean felt restless due to difficulty in breathing and chest pain. Felt something very suspicious and called the ambulance immediately, got admitted to a nearby hospital. After a number of tests, it was found that he had a minor heart attack and was required to have bypass surgery within two days.

I visited him along with the cardiology team. The cardiology team explained to him the entire process of cardiac surgery in detail and he was asked to call family members or any relative to sign the consent form. Mr Jame looked at us and said that he is alone in this world, with absolutely no blood relation of his own, no parents, no siblings, no kids or wife.

He was a 45 years old man with such a high-profile job as per the personal records but has no one to call his family or friends. The chief surgeon suggested that he should call his close friends in the situation where he denied the same. He shared that every three years his job please changes and never gets to me thanks anyway. He added that he never believed his colleagues to be his friends. With a sad smile on his face, Mr Jame said that he has only had a dog to call his good friend for the past 10 years. Mr James asked the surgeon to start the surgery and confirm that if anything happens to him during the surgery his entire wealth and belongings will be given to the "trust for the poor".

The surgery was successful but he landed in post-surgical problems including weakness, blood pressure fluctuation and major scars. After his discharge, he was assigned to visit my clinic for cardiac rehabilitation. It is basically a process to help people get back to their normal day-to-day life with some exercises and body movements.

During his visit to my clinic, he expressed his loneliness and sadness in life. He said he felt so lonely during this time because there was no one to ask about his health, take care of his medicines, and make him food with love and concern. Only his dog was there to keep his eyes on his master.

Mr Jame confessed that he never appreciated and took his life or health seriously. His major goal in life was to make more money and spend it on drinking and smoking. With his attitude and anger issues, he never made friends and even built bridges with his loved ones. He said that when he was in the hospital he was asking for forgiveness from God for not taking his health, relationships or life goals seriously. His only wish was to have his loved ones near him when he was in death bed. Fortunately, he did very well and became better with rehabilitation which actually changed his perspective on life. After getting recovered and being discharged from the rehabilitation center, he changed his job and left the country.

From this encounter with Mr Jame. I learnt that money is or should not be the only goal in your life. "We need to understand the importance of our health, and loved ones in life. We all look at the world from our own window. But doctors look at the world from a patient's window that can teach a lot about life."

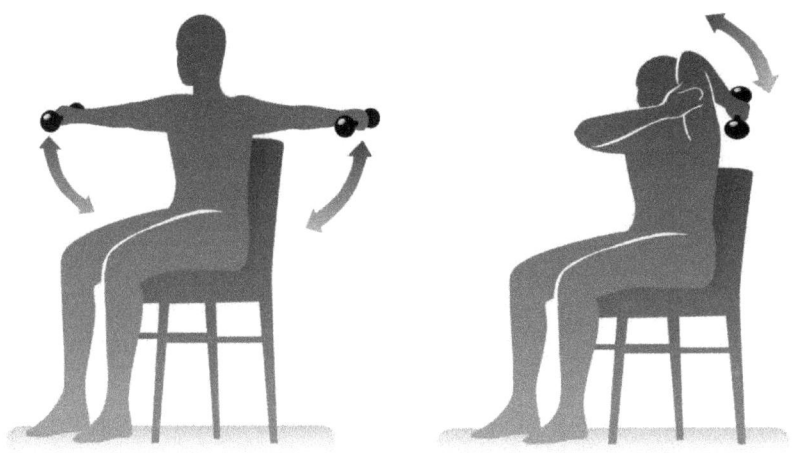

Strength training

Stretching and flexibility

Fig. 1.1 Suggested exercises for body strength and flexibility

Take-Homes from This Chapter

No matter what kind of money you have, your relationships define your final moments on your deathbed be happy or sad.

People who use their extra potential stimulation can beat any hard situation in life and find the solution out of the box.

Death is the ultimate end point of any living creature but to live a life worthy is in purely your hand. Train your body and mind to withstand situations and stay active to keep your health in check.

Daily body movement is as important as eating food to your body. To escape those long-term medications or surgeries, rehabilitation is the only way.

CHAPTER 2

The Secret of Fitness from Childhood to Old Age

Fitness is a journey and not a destination.

There are limitless benefits of fitness from childhood to old age. Every day there is a new opportunity and one has to make the most of it. It has been observed that children who start getting trained for intense exercises at a very early stage of their life, for example, tennis, gymnastics, or any other sports, tend to have a different pattern of life. Their genes express themselves very differently that stay with them for the longest in their lives. Scientists have found evidence of benefits related to exercise and the early age of human beings. These benefits get passed on by mothers who exercise regularly during their pregnancy or even before their newborns' conception.

Yet given the mother sharing her circulation with the offspring within the body, all kinds of changes are passed on in terms of hormonal or gene levels. This not only affects their health but also increases their energy efficiency and muscle health which benefit them throughout their lives. Physical fitness in walls the performance of the heart, lungs, and muscles of the body. Fitness influences the quality of mental and emotional stability up to some extent.

Fitness is not only linked with a structured or shaped body but stands for the condition of being physically and mentally healthy. It is the ability to carry out daily tasks with energy and happiness.

I am going to share the five physical fitness mantras with you.

1. Body Composition

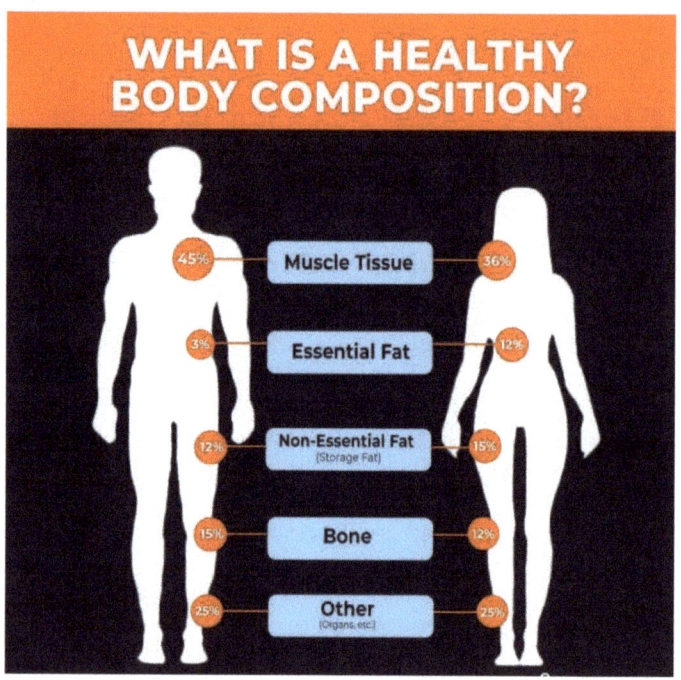

Fig. 2.1 Body composition

The composition of the body determines the percentage of your total weight of body coming from fat, muscles, and bones. Being a word about your body composition and providing more detailed information regarding your overall health. This can be better understood by taking the example of two people with the same body weight but have different fitness and health requirements. This varies due to different body compositions and different bodies. Maintaining a healthy body composition is very important for your health in order to let your body walk under any circumstances.

2. Flexibility

Being flexible does not only define your overall physical activity performance but also increases your activeness. This also reduces the risk of injuries taking longer to recover, and helps each and every joint of your body move through the full range of motion. Health flexibility is basically the ability of your joints or a group of joints to move through a pain-free and unrestricted motion. Also, we can note that the flexibility degree or level varies from person to person depending upon their daily movement practices. A flexible body is one of the major sources of keeping your mind healthy and happy. Basic stretches or yoga are best for beginners to try in order to increase their body flexibility.

Fig 2.2 Flexibility

3. Muscular Strength

Muscular strength helps you get better with your body weight by burning calories and enhancing your body composition. In simple words, this is the degree or the amount of force you can put out a weight. It is the ratio of your fat and muscle that varies from person to person as per their daily routine and exercises. Building your muscle strength can also make a huge difference in your mood changes and energy levels with the help of a healthy sleep pattern.

Fig 2.3 Muscular strength

To increase your muscle strength, you can start with beginner-friendly exercises including push-ups such as incline push-ups or wall/bench push-ups, squads yeah, and climbing stairs.

4. Muscular Endurance

Muscular endurance defines how many times you can move apart kilo weight without getting tired or exhausted. The ability of muscles to make regular contractions against the force for a long time makes you healthy within. Improved body composition also helps you maintain perfect muscular endurance.

Fig 2.4 Muscular endurance

Greater muscular endurance allows a person to complete more repetitions of an exercise, for example, push-ups or squats. You can increase your muscular endurance by including some basic exercises in your daily routine for example cycling, swimming, dancing or system, and walking and running.

5. Cardio-Respiratory Endurance

Cardiorespiratory endurance, a crucial sign of physical health, is the capacity of the heart and lungs to supply oxygen-rich blood to working muscles throughout prolonged physical exercise. Exercises that rely on cardiorespiratory endurance include cycling, swimming, and strenuous long-distance running. This fitness factor also has an impact on a person's capacity to carry out less strenuous, prolonged whole-body tasks like brisk walking, stair climbing, and household chores without experiencing getting tired or restless.

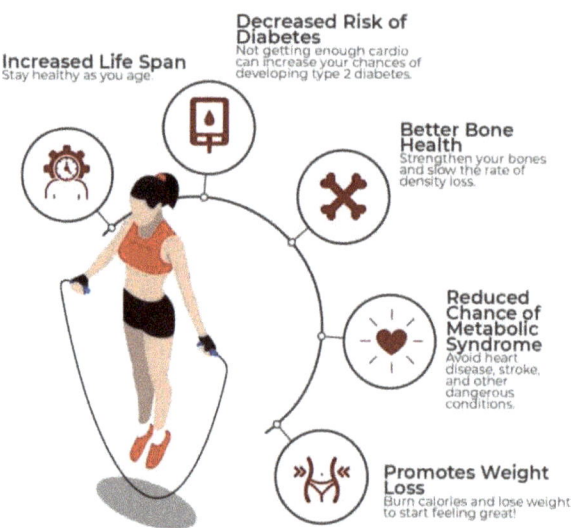

Fig 2.5 Cardio-respiratory endurance

Lazy child syndrome

Inflated self-esteem, a powerful sense of entitlement, and parents who demand little and expect even less are the signs of your kid being lazy. These children lack a feeling of worldly curiosity and show little interest in the majority of activities. They like low-effort pursuits since they tend to be somewhat docile.

They anticipate being amused or receiving stuff to keep them occupied and content. Exasperating youngsters like this exist. Motivating yourself is the key to combating lethargy. If laziness originated from a lack of drive, there must be a cause. These causes can be attributable to worry brought on by prior disappointment and despair.

Children that react poorly to these characteristics may have a hard time recovering. Even if you as a parent frequently think you are inspiring your child, do you realise you could have been going about it incorrectly? It's possible that there are better methods to help your sluggish child change his or her attitude about work, grow more curious about the world, learn to accept responsibility, and eventually succeed in whatever it is that they set out to do in life.

I would like to give some tips to those parents on how they can deal with such kids:

Make them aware of how things don't come from their comfort zone and that they have to work to get things done.

Be an example for them of doing hard work to achieve something. They will learn from you than getting schooled.

Ask them to help you with your chores and have expectations. Discuss that expectation with them in order to make them understand that they need to work for the same.

Note: A child is a student who learns everything first from their parents themselves. Make sure to teach him/her the best you can.

One more story needs to added which is mail annexure 1

Relation between a fit & healthy body self-steem

In a regular rehab program, I met a six years old girl named Sana. She was Found overweight for her age. She had a flat foot and a low tendency to walk as compared to normal kids. She was in a regular rehabilitation program with me. One day I met her mother and she complained that Sana does not want to go to school. She was very sad and low on energy. Later on, after having a discussion with her teachers and principals, we got to know that she was being bullied by other kids due to her weight.

Kids called her "potato" and that made her feel very low in confidence. She lost her self-esteem due to which she was depressed and even refused to go to school. This incident was not only lowering her self-esteem but also making her underconfident and lazy. But with the help of a rehab program and counseling, she started gaining her confidence back.

During that time only, I was helping another boy named Vivek, 12 years old from seventh standard, who was a slow learner, obese, and with very low self-esteem. During this training, I observed that the boy was mentally alert and smart enough to get trained and score well in academics. Whereas it was also said that being overweight made him bullied by other classmates and school kids which made him depressed and low esteemed. He had very few new friends but with the advice of a weight loss program after which he became fit and able to maintain his weight after which he started focusing on his studies and scored well. We can clearly mention that this fitness journey of oil has changed a lot in Vivek's life.

How parenting affects your kids and their mental state

The journey of a good and healthy mindset should start from early childhood and be an ongoing process. This can only be developed as a habit for their child's parents to not only give lectures about being fit but also do it themselves. This will create an example for kids to develop good habits of staying fit in life. The responsibility of parents not only includes bringing up their child but also practising mindful parenting from day one. I'm going to share a story of a 7-year-old kid, Aditya, from the second standard.

A few years back I was a part of a school panel to help slow loudness learners in order to integrate and participate them in the normal stream of education. During that time one primary teacher started complaining about the seven-year-old kid regarding his misbehaviour and use of bad words. He was very aggressive and abusive which affected a lot of other kids as well. Aditya had a bad habit of using bad words and language in an ugly manner. His parents and teachers made him understand yeah with love and punishment but nothing really helped. A school counsellor and I were assessed to help the child in this matter.

It was observed that this behaviour of Aditya was acquired from his parents themselves. His father was abusive and aggressive with his mother at home. The boy copied the exact behaviour thinking that this is the correct way of managing fights. His parents were called by the school and sent to the psychologist for family counselling. They were made to understand how important is it for the parents to develop the right environment for the kid to not indulge in any bad behaviour or personality.

Things to Keep in Mind about Your Body and Its Maintenance

1. Height-Weight Charts

A person's weight is linked with the weight of that person. The chart given below is an ideal height-weight calculation for an individual.

Height		Weight	
		Men (kg)	Women (kg)
5' 0"	(152 Cm)	50 - 54	48 - 52
5' 1"	(155 Cm)	52 - 56	50 - 54
5' 2"	(157 Cm)	54 - 58	51 - 55
5' 3"	(160 Cm)	56 - 60	53 - 57
5' 4"	(163 Cm)	57 - 61	55 - 59
5' 5"	(165 Cm)	59 - 63	57 - 61
5' 6"	(168 Cm)	61 - 65	58 - 62
5' 7"	(170 Cm)	63 - 67	60 - 64
5' 8"	(173 Cm)	65 - 69	62 - 66
5' 9"	(176 Cm)	67 - 71	64 - 68
5' 10"	(177 Cm)	69 - 73	66 - 70
5' 11"	(180 Cm)	71 - 75	68 - 72
6' 0"	(183 Cm)	73 - 77	70 - 74
6' 1"	(185 Cm)	75 - 79	72 - 76
6' 2"	(188 Cm)	77 - 81	74 - 78
6' 3"	(181 Cm)	80 - 84	78 - 80

Fig 2.6 Height-weight chart

2. BMI

Body mass index (BMI) is a person's weight in kilograms (or pounds) divided by the square of height in meters (or feet). A high BMI can indicate high body fat. BMI screens for weight categories that may lead to health problems, but it does not diagnose the body fatness or health of an individual.

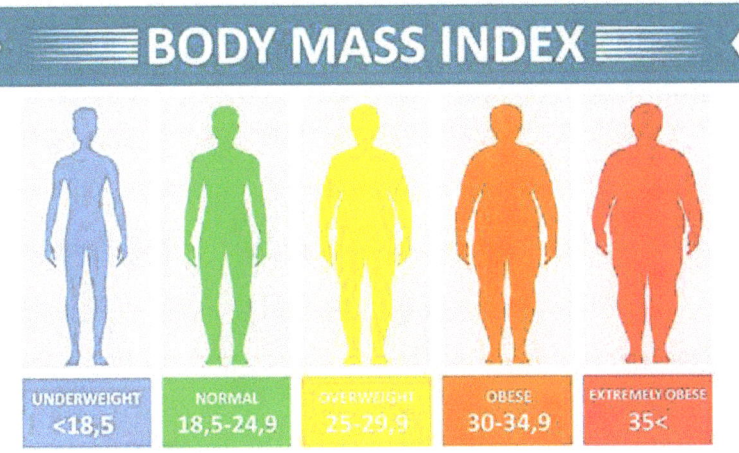

Fig 2.7 BMI

3. Growth Measurement of Various Parts of the Body

Table 2.1 Growth measurement of various parts of the body

Characters	Mean (% in HL)	SD (% in HL)	Mean (% in SL)	SD (% in SL)
Eye diameter	14.34	2.01	14.34	2.01
Interorbital width	11.9	1.27	11.9	1.27
Preorbital	11.97	0.52	11.97	0.52
Postorbital	18.73	1.13	18.73	1.13
Analspine length	7.15	1.05	7.15	1.05
Ist dorsal fin height	8.2	0.82	8.2	0.82
IInd dorsal fin height	14.37	0.97	14.37	0.97
IIIrd dorsal fin height	16.31	1.02	16.31	1.02
IVth dorsal fin height	13.06	0.92	13.06	0.92
Vth dorsal fin height	9.36	0.43	9.36	0.43
VIth dorsal fin height	6.07	0.81	6.07	0.81
Pelvic fin length	15.89	0.68	15.89	0.68
Pectoral fin length	24.15	1.18	24.15	1.18
Height of caudal peduncle	10.78	0.67	10.78	0.67
Caudal peduncle length	22.86	2.26	22.86	2.26
Anal fin length	14.67	0.5	14.67	0.5
Body depth	41.44	1.87	41.44	1.87
Anal length			69.39	1.66

4. WHR

The waist-to-hip ratio (WHR) looks at the proportion of fat stored on your body around your waist and hip. It is a simple but useful measure of fat distribution. WHR is calculated by dividing your waist measurement by your hip measurement since the hips are the widest part of your buttocks.

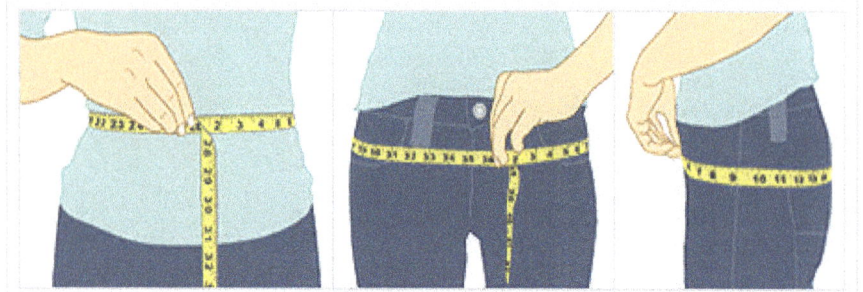

Fig 2.8 Waist/ hip ratio

5. Aerobic Exercises

Exercise that relies mostly on the cardiovascular energy-generating mechanism is referred to as aerobic exercise. According to the dictionary, the term "aerobic" refers to the utilization of oxygen to appropriately provide the energy demands of aerobic metabolism during activity. Repeated sequences of light-to-moderate exercise intensities over an extended period of time are known as aerobic exercises. Since aerobic activity is intended to be low-intensity enough that all carbohydrates are aerobically converted into energy via mitochondrial ATP generation, it may be more accurate to refer to it as "solely aerobic." Oxygen is required by mitochondria for the metabolism of carbohydrates, proteins, and lipids. Medium- to long-distance running or jogging, swimming, cycling, stair climbing, and walking are a few examples of cardiovascular or aerobic exercise.

Fig 2.9 Aerobic exercises

Aerobic exercises help your body strengthen the muscles, improve circulation, increase pain tolerance and reduce the risk of cardiac arrest. This also helps your body recover from any injury in less time than usual.

Take-Homes for Readers

Stay active and include daily movement in your daily routine.

Be a mindful parent while raising a kid because they learn what you do.

Keep a check on your kids, and know what they go through in their surroundings and schools.

Maintain body composition, and do mild exercises to keep your body healthy and in shape.

Questions for You:

Q1: Why is it important for children to engage in regular physical activity and maintain a healthy level of fitness?

Q2: How does a lack of physical fitness in old age affect quality of life and overall health?

Q3: How does regular physical activity and fitness affect cognitive development in children?

Q4: How can older adults benefit from staying physically fit and active in their later years?

CHAPTER 3

Exercise Happiness Paradox

Unlocking Mental Strength through Positive Mindset

Right Mental Attitude

Studies show what a good or bad diet does to one's body, and what positive or negative thoughts do to one's mind. Feed your mind with positive thoughts and you'll start seeing amazing changes in your life.

A happy mindset influences many decisions that people make. It encourages people to have better relationships with themselves, others, and the unknown. Spirituality can help you deal with stress by giving you a sense of peace, purpose, and forgiveness. It often becomes more important in times of emotional stress or illness.

Once you change your perspective and start thinking positively, your mind will be clear of any negativity. You'll find yourself viewing the world in a new light. You'll stop blaming yourself or others. Your emotions will be controllable, and you'll try to seek value from every setback you experience.

Impact of Healthy Mental Health on Your Body

Here are a few more reasons why you should have a positive and healthy mental attitude:

Happiness

A positive attitude is known to be linked with a feeling of happiness. There are also many external factors that can contribute to happiness, but it starts from within. Emotions like joy and contentment come from a sense of peace and joy, which can happen irrespective of the situation you are in. To put it simply, you can be happy right now if you think positively.

Self-Confidence

It's impossible to feel confident if you don't truly love yourself, which is why we recommend taking the time on a regular basis to do so. You'll treat yourself with more respect and appreciation and the more you do this, the more confident you'll become in your persona. This will lead you to successfully take on new challenges, breaking through self-limiting beliefs.

Training Your Mind to Develop a Positive Attitude

Repeating positive affirmations and reading inspirational quotes daily can be a great way to train your mind to think positively. If you are having a hard time with negative thoughts or feeling down, just remember that your goals are within reach. You just have to believe in them. Whenever you have a negative thought, replace it with a positive one. Even when situations may seem dire, a positive mindset will help you move through them more easily.

The Mantra of Happiness

A person with a happy mood and mindset can do things that a person with a bad mood and mindset couldn't!

Here, I'm sharing the hormone responsible for your actions and how you can maintain those with some minimal steps. I hope it'll help you!

Dopamine **(The reward chemical)**	**Oxytocin** **(The love hormone)**
Completing a task (accomplishment) Self-care or spending time with yourself Eating comfort food Celebrating little wins	Playing with babies/pets Warm and gentle hugs from loved ones Holding hands Giving/receiving compliments
Serotonin **(The mood stabilizer)**	**Endorphin** **(The pain killer)**
Meditating/running Sun exposure Swimming/cycling	Exercising Laughter therapy Essentials oils/dark chocolate

Table 3.1 Hormone Results for Your Actions

The time bank

In Switzerland, there is a concept named "Time bank" has been imposed on citizens to save their time as a currency where they can deposit and withdraw time when needed. The Swiss Ministry of health created the time bank concept as an old-age assistance programme under which people can volunteer to look. After elderly people who require assistance and then the number of hours. They spend with us and get a deposit in their individual. Social security account.

Eventually, when the volunteer reaches us at old age, and when she or he requires what the time Bank could help them. Basically time, Bank is a barter system that allows people to deposit and withdraw that time, based on their abilities and needs, for example, women, setting, gardening, teaching or supporting old citizens. This is really a great and important concept as I remembered the story regarding the same.

I remember when I visited a ward where a very old lady used to sit alone in the corner in a wheelchair. I was told that she was 92 years old and terminally ill and very few months were left in her life. She was very lonely as a new visitor, or her own. Children had visited her past five years. I visited her one fine morning just to ask. How can I help her? She looked at me and smile while Singh inverted, can you hug me and hold my hand so sometimes" I was surprised. Apparently, her own son and daughter had never visited her for the past five years. She used to get Christmas cards from her children.

I gave her a warm hug, kissed on her cheeks, and held her hand for some time. She was very happy and whispered. Thanks, in my ears with every ice. I thought if the "time bank" concept would have been there that time, she could have used it now for her.

On the other hand, I thought of my mother in India, who was surrounded by many people like her own kids, neighbors, friends, helpers, and relatives. Without even asking for their attention, she got all of it. That is incredible and amazing about India where relationships are valued and maintained with respect and love.

Mugdha and Her "Out of the Box" Painting

Understand your kids!

My seven-year-old daughter, Mugdha, was excellent in drawing, studies, and sports. From the age of 4, she used to receive the first prize in drawing competitions. Thinking of the same, I took her out for a competition when she was seven years old to compete with other 50 kids, where the subject of the competition was "a sweet home."

Each and every kid there was trained with so much focus and concentration but my focus was on my daughter assuming that she will the first prize in this competition as well. But when the price was announced and she could not make it too seem that made her very upset and even I thought of scolding her for the same. But before that, I approached the examiner and asked her to show what she has shown. The examiner asked Mugdha to explain her painting where she has drawn a very tiny house surrounded by trees and grass.

She explained that this is her point of view of seeing her house from an aeroplane that is up in the sky and far away from the house. This made me and the examiner shocked realizing how a seven-year-old had thought out of the box to draw something. Not to forget that the examiner gives her a small gift to appreciate her idea and that they decided to understand her thought process from her perspective and not mine. This made me realize the importance of understanding your kid and not just concluding by seeing their actions.

Understanding them is very important before making any decision based on their actions that definitely have some significance in their own mind. Yeah, this acknowledgment from her examiner made her self-esteemed, confident and focused through various activities in life. Yes, of course, I got to learn a lot from this.

Research

Recent research indicates that religious practices and beliefs help people deal with life's stresses and are good for their mental health. Our patients place a significant value on religious beliefs and practices. Existential concerns may be the root of many of their issues. Therefore, it is essential that we incorporate religious and spiritual practices into our treatment plan (Grover et al., 2020). In our approach to psychiatry, we must propagate the Bio-psycho-socio-spiritual model.

Psychiatry's predominant position has always been that it has nothing to do with spirituality or religion. Psychiatrists have viewed religious practices and beliefs in this light for more than a century. For a long time, it has been believed that they have a pathological basis. Religion was regarded as a mental illness symptom (Abbas et al., 2021).

However, recent studies strongly suggest that for many patients, religion and spirituality are tools for coping with life's stresses, including those caused by their illnesses. Nowadays, a lot of psychiatrists think that religion and spirituality are important for their patients' lives. The significance of otherworldliness in emotional well-being is currently broadly acknowledged. Akbari & Hossaini (2018) state that effective psychiatric practice necessitates religious-psychiatric reconciliation.

Making Big Changes in Life by Taking Small Steps Every day!

One can easily make a big difference in their life by taking small steps every day for 365 days. In order to create a huge impact, you need to start with that one block to build a castle. Here's how you can do it.

Start small: Start with 5 minutes' walk/yoga a day and make it to 15 minutes and eventually an hour as the days pass by.

Set actionable goals: Don't go for cliché, overachieving goal setting. Look at what's best suitable for you and your body and create actionable goals.

Take out time (responsibly): You need to take your routine seriously and stop saying "I'm too busy to do so".

Be prepared: Brainstorm to eliminate those obstacles (excuses) and take every step with a smile.

Define your "why" and "how": Unless you have a purpose, there's no point in doing all this.

Keep it interesting: Keep changing your exercises or music track to make it more interesting.

Learn what works for 'you': Note down what worked well and what didn't work for you throughout the process.

Enjoy the process: Don't just do it for the sake of doing it but enjoy the entire journey.

Get a pace and there you go!

Take-Home Messages

Those with a positive attitude are more energetic and stronger. A positive attitude can contribute to positive health effects as well; stress levels lower and your general well-being improves.

Fitness is not a destination but rather a way of life a story. This does not only mean physical appearance but also mental health.

Even in the toughest times, choose to be happy and optimistic. When things don't go as planned, instead of being stressed out about it, work hard towards your goals with a positive attitude and you will see amazing progress.

A child's physical and mental health are both equally important as off and adults. If that is taken care of properly, the fitness journey becomes smooth for them towards their old age. Parents' support and encouraging words could help their children develop self-confidence and high self-esteem to maintain a healthy emotional outlook.

Questions for You

Q1: How does regular physical activity impact one's emotional state and overall happiness?

Q2: What are some potential explanations for the exercise-happiness paradox?

Q3: How does exercise interact with other factors, such as social support, to influence our happiness?

Q4: How can we measure the impact of exercise on happiness in a scientific way?

Q5: How does the relationship between exercise and happiness vary among different individuals and populations?

CHAPTER 4

Health span vs Life span and Exercise Science

The Science of Exercise and Health for a Vital Future

Every human being should carefully think about the above saying. In the recent era, there is a drastic increase in the world's population. Hence, life expectancy has increased from 47 years to 73 years which is good news. The entire phase from birth to death can be divided into two parts called the life span and health span. You all might be aware of the lifespan as it is a common word used by everyone. Life span is the total life lived by a person. Then what is health span? A health span is defined as a total period lived free from diseases.

So, before moving on let us understand what is aging and does everyone age. The answer is yes! Everyone will experience the process of aging but not in the same way. Aging completely depends on the lifestyle of an individual. Although there is a difference between age and aging. Aging can be described as the time-related decline of psychological and physiological processes required for survival and reproduction. It is the universal process that started with the genesis of life whereas age is the chronological advancement of time.

Nowadays we can see an increasing number of individuals surviving old age and spending long years at later ages which is clear that longevity or a biological aging process is taking place. But the real question to ask ourselves is, **are we aging healthy?** Even though individuals reach the age of 93, they still face death due to being bedridden, low quality of life, or due to mobility issues. Thereby, currently, the overall assessment of health and lifestyle is crucial. Proper planning of health should be taken care of by every individual in order to have a good health span.

There is widespread consensus that extending the time of life spent in excellent health is important due to the substantial economic and social advantages. The change in health due to aging can be due to physiological dysregulation, as evidenced by a variety of biological risk factors, preceding the late diagnosis of illnesses, loss of functioning and impairment, frailty, and finally mortality associated with aging. A decline in cognitive functioning is also one of the reasons for the deterioration of health during the aging process ("National Institute on Aging (NIA)," 2008)

Exercise Science

Now I want to bring your attention to the term Exercise Science. It is a field that seeks to comprehend and enhance individual well-being via the implementation of solutions to health issues associated with physical inactivity. Real aging sets in with a decline in musculoskeletal and cognitive function affecting the overall physical and mental balance.

Regular exercise has been shown to lessen the physiological impacts of a sedentary lifestyle, hence increasing active life expectancy and decreasing the risk of developing and progressing chronic diseases and debilitating disorders.

Physical activity and exercise

Some changes associated with aging, such as wrinkles and grey hair, are unavoidable. Once upon a time, it was believed that modifications in muscles, bones, and joints were also inevitable. However, researchers now believe that many of the characteristics linked with aging are the result of inactivity, and that physical exercise may help decrease or eliminate the risk of impairment and chronic illness.

Regular exercise may reduce the negative physical, emotional, and cognitive impacts of aging, but it cannot stop the biological aging process. Increasing physical activity beginning in midlife and continuing into old age lowers the risk of chronic disease and death. In addition to preventing cardiovascular and metabolic diseases, physical exercise may also minimize the risk of dementia and preserve cognitive function. Neurological senescence may be delayed by regular exercise, and the brain regions particularly impacted by the aging process may benefit the most.

Regular physical activity is one of the most essential things that we need to do for healthy living as we get older. It may prevent or postpone the onset of several age-related health issues. It also helps the muscles develop stronger, allowing us to continue doing daily tasks without becoming dependent on others.

Aerobic activity, muscular building activities, and flexibility exercises are beneficial for the elderly and should be included in a fitness program. In addition to the other aspects of health-related physical fitness, those who are at risk for falling or mobility loss should practice activities designed to enhance balance

Move More and Sit Less

Throughout the day, older people must try to move more and sit less. Always keep in mind that any kind of physical activity is always better than none. Those over 60 who reduce their sitting time and increase their moderate-to-vigorous activity levels will see further improvements in their health.

One must do activities that can strengthen the muscles at least twice every week. These sorts of exercises can assist you to maintain muscle mass as you age. Be it at home or at the gym, you have several options for gaining muscle mass. You should do moves that work your major muscle groups (the legs, hips, back, chest, belly, shoulders, and arms).

The Balancing Act

Balance issues grow increasingly prevalent with aging. Loss of musculoskeletal function leads to loss of balance. Most commonly falls are associated with balance issues in persons over 65 years of age. Each year, one-third of persons in this age bracket and more than half of those older than 75 can lose balance. Both men and women are similarly impacted. Therefore, balance is a vital component of exercise, particularly for elderly persons and those with difficulty moving.

Maintaining your balance and performing balance-related exercises as you age and understanding how to avoid falls may help you do everyday tasks by moving about freely without any support and depending less on others. Tai chi, walking backward, and practicing standing on one leg are examples of balance-improving activities. A loss of balance can sometimes have a very bad impact on the lifestyle as you get older.

Walking and Aging Slow

When you hear the term walking the first thing that comes to your mind is your leg! Many older adults believe that movement of the legs is very much required in order to walk. However, it's the other way around. Walking is essential to preserve the movement of your legs.

Scientists have identified a probable association between walking and biological age. It is proven that the biological aging process may be slowed by brisk walking. I-Min Lee, a professor at the Department of Epidemiology, discovered that elderly women who walk at least 4,400 steps per day live longer than those who walk less.

You often tend to ignore your feet as you get older. A decrease in the proportion of leg muscles and stiff joints is the result of long-term inactivity in the legs. Hence constant leg movement or exercise should become a necessary part of your daily life in order to retain the strength in the muscles thereby leading to healthy aging.

Research findings indicate that inactivity has the same effect on the physical strength of young and elderly men. Young individuals lose up to one-third of their muscle power after having one leg immobilized for two weeks, while elderly persons lose around one-fourth. A young man who is immobile for two weeks loses muscle power in his leg comparable to aging by 40 or 50 years (Vigelsø et al., 2015)

Physical inactivity is a significant secondary factor that influences muscle aging. You often forget that the entire body is balanced by the legs. The largest and strongest bones and joints are also present in the legs and 70 percent of human activity is carried out by the legs. Hence only with regular strengthening of the legs, one can reduce the risk of an aging-related serious conditions such as a disability.

With this context, I would like to share one of my own life lessons which is connected to my late mother.

> Most of the time we understand the real value of aging when we see our loved ones go through the process of aging. During my career of practicing, I have come across many elderly patients and have successfully and efficiently treated most of them. But, I still get emotionally disturbed when I think about the death of my own mother. I feel that I never gave enough attention to her health. My mother expired at the age of 84 but sad to say that she was dysfunctional for seven years prior to her death and she almost started losing the strength in her legs when she was around 70 years old. But, as I was based in Dubai I was not able to attend to her often when she needed me the most.
>
> Every single year her health declined very badly. At the age of 75, she was already struggling to walk without support and unfortunately at the age of 78, she had a fractured hip due to a fall. However, she had a successful hip replacement but to her bad luck, she completely lost strength in both her legs forever. Thus, she was bedridden during her last five years. I now regret that I could have easily avoided my mother from becoming bedridden only if I had helped her in strengthening her leg muscles well in advance.

Upon reviewing several such instances, I have seen a rise in longevity, which is defined as the duration of life beyond the control of the biological aging process. however, the productive years before death are bad and are really scary to even think about. Hence from the above life story, I would like to stress and recommend that there is an immediate need for you to keep your body functional all the time which in turn can improve the quality of life when the aging process sets in.

"In the end, it's not the years in your life that counts. It's the life in your years'.'

One should never forget this famous quote by Abraham Lincoln which ultimately reminds us about healthy aging. However, you often ignore the importance of mental health and concentrate only on staying physically active. Mental illness has been one of the major age-related problems, especially depression, and dementia. There is evidence that says that both physical and mental conditions are interconnected.

Risk Factors for Mental Health Problems among Older Adults

One's susceptibility to mental health problems might be heightened at any moment by a number of factors. Stresses that are more frequent in later age, such as a major continuous loss of abilities and a reduction in functional capacity, may add an extra layer of difficulty to an already challenging existence for the elderly.

Some of the many reasons the elderly may need constant attention include mobility problems, chronic pain, frailty, and so on. Additionally, the elderly are disproportionately affected by depression and economic loss. People of advanced age who are vulnerable to the negative effects of these pressures, such as social isolation, loneliness, or mental agony, may need long-term care.

There is a correlation between the presence of a physical health issue, such as heart disease, and an increased risk of depression in older persons. Also, the prognosis for an elderly person's cardiac condition might be worsened by untreated depression.

Physical, verbal, financial, and psychological violence; abandonment; negligence; and severe losses of respect and dignity are all forms of elder abuse. Negative effects on mental health, such as depression and anxiety, may be just as damaging to an older victim of abuse as physical injury.

Therefore, training your body and mind is essential if you want to keep a steady link between your brain and your muscles (TYBM). If you don't put in the time and effort to develop both your physical and mental capabilities, you won't be able to realize your full potential. God created a day with 24 hours in it. Still, it's up to you to figure out how to make the most of your day. Either you put that time to good use, or you squander it and gain nothing. That's why I developed a program called Train Your Body & Mind, through which people can improve their physical health to the fullest extent possible by developing their attitudes towards the health span Hence following TYBM (Train Your Body & Mind) can have a great impact on your lifestyle.

Let us see how an individual can implement TYBM. I have mentioned a few techniques below which can help you train both your body and mind.

Table 4.1 TYBM techniques

TRAIN YOUR BODY & MIND (TYBM)	
Mindfulness	Helps in slowing down the heart rate, calming the breath, and relaxing the body.
Meditation	Helps the body relax and manages depression and anxiety issues
Relaxation techniques and self-care	There are many relaxation therapies available that can help in reducing both physical and mental stress.
Yoga, Tai Chi, and Qigong	All these three techniques use slow body movements which help in mental relaxation and reduce physical stress.

Other activities like reading papers or magazines, playing games, stitching, or developing new hobbies and skills are equally important for maintaining a healthy mind and body.

Energy Systems: Understanding Exercise

Once you start exercising you should be aware of bodily movements and understand how your body responds to the activity. Hence having basic knowledge about the process of exercise and its effects on the body is crucial. Your body requires energy in order to perform some exercise. In scientific language that energy is known as ATP (Adenosine Triphosphate).

As you know the body obtains energy in the form of ATP from the breakdown of food or macronutrients such as proteins, carbohydrates, and fats. This ATP acts as a fuel for bodily movements such as muscle contraction. However, the availability of ATP is limited hence the body has to obtain it from other sources known as **energy systems**. Hence for better understanding, I have provided information on the energy system in tabular format. Table - 2 gives information on the different types of energy systems are the three energy systems of the human body and Table-3 provides a summary of the differences between aerobic and anaerobic exercises.

Table 4. 2: Energy systems involved in different physical activities

Energy system	Oxygen requirement	Exercise Performance Time	Examples of activity
The phosphagen system / ATP-PC system	No	<10 secs	weightlifting, short sprints, or throwing a ball
ATP-PC and lactic acid system	No	10 - 90 secs	sprinting, high-intensity interval training (HIIT), power-lifting, swimming
The Oxidative System / Aerobic System	Yes	More than 3 mins	walking, jogging, swimming, biking and jumping rope

Table 4.3: Difference between aerobic and anaerobic exercise

Aerobic exercise	Anaerobic exercise
Low to moderate level of exercise	Higher intensity workouts
Can be sustained through a longer duration	Short duration (Intervals)
Increases the heart rate gradually	Increases heart rate very quickly
Oxygen is being utilized as a fuel for muscles	Oxygen is absent and glycogen is utilized

Various physical activities use different energy systems. Activities performed in less than 10 seconds like throwing and jumping make use of the phosphagen energy system. Weight lifting and other sports require an anaerobic energy system. Exercises like walking and running make use of the aerobic system for the supply of energy. Here's a breakdown by the sport/activity of the relative importance (in percentage) of different energy sources.

Table 4.4: Percentage contribution of the different energy system to various sports/ activities

Sports/ Activity	ATP-PC System	ATP-PC and Lactic acid system	Aerobic System
Walking	0	5	95
Hockey	50	20	30
Basketball	60	20	20
Swimming	10	20	70

Golf Swing	95	5	0
Running	10	20	70
Football	90	10	0
Tennis	70	20	10

Fuel and Muscle Type

Phosphocreatine (PCr), carbohydrates in the form of glycogen replenishment, blood glucose, fat in the form of triacylglycerol, non-esterified fatty acids (NEFA), and ketone bodies, are the three principal substrates for ATP resynthesis during muscle contraction. Oxidative metabolism in muscle tissue relies mostly on fat and carbs as fuels.

Glycogenolysis was formerly thought to be the first step in muscle contraction fueling when it was shown in exercise science that PCr was the sole fuel utilized at the outset of muscular contraction. However, several research investigations have shown that ATP resynthesis from glycolysis occurs practically immediately at the beginning of the activity, especially during the 30 seconds of intense activity (Henriksson, 1995).

The only source of energy for muscle contraction is adenosine triphosphate (ATP). However, the amount of ATP available in mammalian skeletal muscle is quite low, and thus it must be constantly regenerated. In human skeletal muscle, ATP resynthesis is entirely fueled by phosphocreatine (PCr), glucose, and fat. However, when the supply of carbohydrates is significantly reduced, amino acid oxidation may contribute marginally to ATP synthesis.

Despite the fact that muscle glycogen is numerically more important as a carbohydrate source of energy for flexing skeletal muscle, blood glucose adds considerably to total carbohydrate metabolism during exercise, particularly during extended, intense activity. But don't rush to the conclusion that training the anaerobic route is your only option if fat-burning and a trimmer physique are your primary objectives. Always keep in mind that the efficacy of one pathway can be improved by training the other and that this applies to the fat-burning benefits of the aerobic and anaerobic pathways alike.

Here is a quick summary of the entire energy system based on the type of fuel required, the intensity, and the duration.

Table 4. 5: Summary of energy systems

Energy system	ATP-PC System	Lactic acid system	Aerobic System
Fuel requirement	Creatine phosphate	Carbohydrate/ glucose from food	Carbohydrates, fats & proteins
Method of energy production	Anaerobic	Anaerobic	Aerobic
Intensity of ATP production	High	Moderate to high	Low
Duration	Less than 10 Seconds (Immediate)	Less than 3 minutes (Short term)	Prolonged/ Continous (Long term)
Ability to contract	Very fast	Fast	Slow

Extra potential stimulation

Each of us was born with a mind that has the capacity to drive us toward our goals. When it comes to our health, however, we tend to be extremely sluggish about realizing our full potential. So, if you want to remain fit and appreciate the ride of your life, it's up to you to unlock that extra potential ability. If you're having trouble accomplishing something, tapping into your hidden potential might be just the thing to push you over the top. Hence, having excellent emotional and physical health is essential if you want to get the most out of your fitness path and your life in general.

Fitness parameters

In today's society, one's physical level is characterized by a slim physique and six-pack abs. Those who meet the criterion are deemed healthy and robust, but others continue to strive for this superficial metric. The fact regarding the level of fitness is that there is no universal standard, and a thin physique is not a criterion for evaluating it.

Some individuals may be genetically skinny yet physically fit in the same way as others. Fitness and lifespan have little to do with physical appearance. Here are 5 ways you must evaluate and strive to improve in order to get more precise results and remain mentally and physically healthy.

- **Stamina:** Stamina is described as the mental and physical capacity to execute a task for a lengthy period of time. It is the capacity to do a task without becoming fatigued.
- **Flexibility:** Flexibility is another essential component of physical fitness. It is the capacity of a muscle or joint to

move across a broad range of motion. Being flexible allows you to engage in daily activities without sustaining injury.

- **Strength**: Having a high level of muscular strength helps prevent your joints from harm while lifting hefty weights on a daily basis. It may improve your balance and lower your chance of falling.

- **Balance:** Balance is described as the body's capacity to avoid falls and maintain its force of gravity throughout a certain activity. It is essential for executing a variety of daily tasks and is especially critical for elderly persons.

- **Posture**: Good posture ensures that your joints and bones are properly aligned. They minimize muscle and ligament wear and breakdown. As you age, slouching, knee locking, and shoulder curving are undesirable body postures that raise the risk of arthritis, osteoporosis, and neck discomfort.

An individual's perceived experience of exercise-induced bodily changes like increased heart rate, breathing rate, sweating, and muscle fatigue is factored into the Borg Rating of Perceived Exertion (RPE). A large amount of apparent exertion is relative to the person judging it. Although the felt exertion measure is subjective, a score between 6 and 20 may be a good estimate of one's actual pulse rate while exercising* (Borg, 2016).

The more you exercise, the more you'll learn to adapt your routine to your body's needs. A "somewhat difficult" ranking on the Borg Scale (typically starting from 6 - 20) would be a good goal for someone strolling for exercise who wants to keep up a moderate level of exertion (12-14). If you're reaching a point of "very moderate" muscle fatigue and breathing during your exercise, you should increase the intensity (score of 9 on the Borg Scale).

If, on the other hand, you evaluated your effort as "highly intense" (19 on the Borg Scale), you may need to tone down your movements to enter the moderate-intensity zone. Below, I have provided Borg's rating scale for your information. Kindly refer to it while starting any exercise.

Table 4.6: Borgs scale

Score	Effort	Description
6	No effort need	Moderate movement, relaxed
7	Extremely light	Can maintain pace
8	Very Light	Can workout comfortably but you start breathing harder
9		
10		
11	Light	Sweating will be minimal and you can talk easily while exercising
12		
13	Somewhat hard	You will experience slight breathlessness however you can still talk
14		Sweating is increased, you can still have a conversation but with difficulty
15	Hard	You continue to sweat and can still push to maintain form
16		

17	Very hard	You can keep a fast pace but only till a shorter period
18		
19	Extremely hard	Having difficulty in breathing and muscle activity will be almost exhausted.
20	Maximally hard	Danger signal and you have to STOP EXERCISING!

MBJTL (Muscles, Bones, Joints, Tendons, and Ligaments)

The musculoskeletal system also weakens with aging. Because of a lack of regular exercise, it is susceptible to deterioration. I have enumerated a few of the age-related alterations that occur in several musculoskeletal system components. But before that, I have given you a short description regarding the MBJTL for a better understanding of their alterations.

Table 4.7: Description of muscle, bones, joints, tendons, and ligaments

Muscles **(M)**	<ul><li>There are a lot of muscles in the body, and they're mostly in the spaces in between the bones.</li><li>Movement, speech, and digestion are all made possible by the body's muscles.</li><li>Muscles of various kinds regulate vital functions such as the pulse, respiration, and metabolism.</li></ul>
Bones **(B)**	<ul><li>Bone is essential for the body's structure and function.</li><li>Humans have 206 bones at maturity.</li><li>They help safeguard vital systems.</li><li>Bones are also the depositary for Minerals</li></ul>

Joints **(J)**	• Joints are the connecting points between two or more bones. • In order to allow the body to move, joints serve their primary purpose. • The purpose of different joints varies with their position.
Tendons **(T)**	• Tendons are flexible connective tissue that link muscle to bone. • Muscles can be attached to other organs, like the eyes, via tendons. • The function of a tendon is to facilitate the movement of a bone or other structural component.
Ligaments **(L)**	• Ligaments are the connective tissue that holds two bones together, most commonly in a joint. • They serve to keep the extremities of two bones together, thereby stabilizing the joint. • It prevents the bones in the joint from bending in an unsafe way or moving too far apart, which could lead to dislocation.

Negative Effects on MBJTL

- **Muscles:** Weakness, exhaustion, and a reduced capacity to tolerate exercise are all possible results of the natural decline in muscle mass that occurs with aging.

- **Bones:** Bone is a kind of living tissue. As you become older, your bones begin to lose their strength and structure. Fractures from falls or even minor knocks are more likely in those with low bone density.

- **Joint:** Within the joints, bones are not in direct touch. The cartilage lining the joint, the synovial membranes surrounding the joint, and the lubricating fluid found inside the joint all work together to keep the joint healthy and functioning (synovial fluid). Joint mobility becomes much more rigid and less flexible as people age because of a decline in lubricating fluid and a thinning of cartilage.

- **Tendons and ligaments:** These connective tissues are regularly organized and serve crucial roles in the preservation of mechanical support and joint mobility. These tissues undergo circulatory and compositional changes as they age, which affect their sequences of interactions between body systems, their biology, healing capability, and biomechanical performance.

However, a lot of these age-related joint changes are a result of inactivity. Increasing one's exercise and movement levels benefit all of these areas. It improves one's efficiency and health by fostering a physique that is both strong and flexible. All of these things deteriorate due to a lack of exercise, as does physical endurance and, consequently, the ability to lead a healthy and productive life. Physical endurance and health aren't the only things that decline; neural, physiological, biochemical, endocrine, and cellular characteristics all suffer as well. To put it simply, you either use it or lose it.

Physical activity may prevent and reverse numerous age-related changes to musculature, bones, and joints. Never is it too late to begin a healthy lifestyle and get its advantages. Below are a few benefits of regular exercise.

- Exercise helps strengthen bones and reduce the pace of bone loss.
- Muscular-strengthening exercises may help the elderly enhance their muscle mass and strength.

- Tai chi and other balance and coordination activities may minimize the chance of falling.
- Physical exercise in old age may postpone the advancement of osteoporosis because it reduces the rate of bone mineral density loss.
- The ideal sort of exercise for maintaining bone mass is a weight-bearing activity, which includes walking or weight training. Twisting or rotating motions in which the muscle connections pull on the bone may also be advantageous.
- Compared to inactive older adults, those who work out in the water (which does not include weight bearing) may nevertheless have improvements in bone and muscle mass.
- Stretching is another wonderful method for preserving joint mobility.

Therefore, to clearly highlight the importance of physical activity in maintaining our health span, I have shared another true story that I came across during my career.

This is a very strange story but it has really made me understand that one has to be active throughout his/her life. The story is about Lata who was my patient for the last 10 years. She was 70 years old and had pain in both her knees. She used to find it very difficult to walk because of the pain in her knees, however, she was able to manage her day-to-day activities.

Unfortunately during the COVID lockdown, she was compelled to stay back at home which made her walk less as she could not go out and it slowly made her lose the confidence to walk alone. Although after COVID she was brought to me for a checkup, sadly she was bound to a wheelchair by then and was unable to walk without the help of a walker or crutches.

Her legs had become very weak and her quality of life also deteriorated. We tried our level best to restore her functioning level but the outcome was really bad. We could observe that at the age of 70, her lifestyle made her live like a 90-year-old woman. Hence, if she could have maintained an active lifestyle by regular exercise right from a young age then she would have easily sustained her leg movements during the COVID pandemic.

Hence, the promotion of physical activity among the elderly is an essential clinical and public health concern. Additionally, exercise helps preserve the body's reflexes and capacity to distribute and use oxygen properly. Incorporating 30 minutes of gentle movement into your everyday routine can have positive health effects.

Take-Home Messages

Walk around, move more, and sit less.

Exercise and train your body and mind (TYBM) simultaneously is one of the best ways to slow down your natural aging process.

Always remember that starting with at least one hour of exercise per day can be your stepping stone to healthy living.

Try to stimulate your extra potential to live a healthy lifestyle and accomplish your desires.

Count your health span and not your life span: Always remember that you have to lead a productive and healthy life as you get older.

Make complete use of Borg's scale and rate yourself while performing the exercise.

Physical and mental fitness is the secret behind healthy aging.

Refer to the fitness parameters and see that your daily exercise helps you attain the parameters in a healthy way.

Ask yourself!

1. Do you follow a healthy lifestyle as you age?
2. Do you practice regular body movements on a day-to-day basis?
3. Are you practicing the exercises for mental health such as mindfulness and relaxation therapies?

4. Do you live your life consciously?
5. Do you understand the importance of MBJTL?
6. Are you monitoring your body with the fitness parameters that are mentioned above?

CHAPTER 5

Fitness Foundation

Die young in mind and body as late as possible.

One of the best things you can do for your health is to engage in regular physical exercise. Physical activity has numerous health benefits, including enhancing cognitive function, aiding in weight management, decreasing the likelihood of developing certain diseases, bolstering the body's immune system, and enhancing mobility and strength.

Some health advantages are associated with reduced sitting time and increased moderate-to-vigorous physical exercise in adults. Physical exercise is one of the few living decisions that can have such a positive effect on health. I will provide an example for you to understand the importance of physical activity.

> Picture yourself waking up at 7 a.m. tomorrow with boundless vitality and anticipation for the day ahead.
>
> The day is yours to do as you please, so you plan to take advantage of it by getting some exercise, strolling around town, and doing some purchasing. You have boundless energy, both emotionally and physically, and you are free from any dependence or limitations.
>
> Now imagine yourself at age 75, still capable of doing all the things that I just listed.

This is the very essence of physical fitness!

All people, regardless of age, ability, race, gender, or height, can reap the health advantages of regular physical exercise. If you want to stay healthy and enjoy a higher standard of living, you should get in shape and learn how much exercise is right for you.

Regular exercise and other forms of physical movement have been shown to enhance health and lower the chance of chronic illnesses like type 2 diabetes, cancer, and heart disease. More significantly, maintaining a daily exercise routine can enhance life satisfaction. These advantages can be yours with as little as 30 minutes of daily effort.

"Exercise hard in silence, let fitness make the noise."

Benefits of Daily Exercise

- You may be able to better control your weight and lower your chance of heart disease if you engage in frequent physical activity.
- You have less chance of getting osteoporosis and sturdier bones, muscles, and ligaments.
- You reduce your potential for falling.
- You feel better, overall, with increased vitality, improved happiness, reduced stress, and improved sleep.

Effect on Mental well-being

- Several investigations have discovered that physical activity is beneficial for depression.
- Working out in a group is a great way to meet new people and socialize.
- Getting fitter might help you feel better emotionally and give you better sleep.
- The brain compounds serotonin, dopamine, and stress factors may all undergo changes as a result of exercise.

Aiming for 30 Minutes a Day

Health experts and academics suggest engaging in moderate-intensity physical exercise for at least 30 minutes on most days, if not all days, in order to keep healthy and lower the chance of health issues.

Strategies to Improve Physical Fitness

Modifying your routine in even seemingly insignificant ways—such as taking the stairs instead of the elevator, parking further away from your destination on the subway or bus, or even just strolling the kids to school—can add up to significant increases in your daily exercise.

Therefore, to consistently exercise and be physically fit the most important thing is to train your body along with your mind (TYBM) and stimulate the extra potential (EPS) which you have. I have a real-life incident to share with you which highlights the importance of TYBM and EPS.

This is the story of a Srilankan girl who not only won the battle over death but also over her quality of life. She taught me how TYBM and EPS work.

Sura was a 25-year-old girl. She met with a very bad van accident along with her husband and other colleagues 6 years ago. Unfortunately, she was crushed very badly in the van seat and was severely injured. She was almost declared dead but still admitted to the hospital. She had multiple fractures in the body but doctors decided not to treat those fractures as saving her life was more important. Other people in the van sustained minor injuries. Sura was in ICU on a ventilator for 3 to 4 months, however, she was non-responsive. The hope of life was minimal. But her luck was really good and the prayers of her parents and family members were answered. Finally, she was out of danger after 4 months of ventilation.

Now the challenge was to treat her fractures which were misaligned. Doctors made a strong decision and started to treat her hip fractures initially followed by other fractures. After prolonged surgeries, doctors realized that she needed extensive rehabilitation as she was hardly able to stand and all her joints had almost fused. After that, she was referred for prolonged rehabilitation. The very first day I met Sura, I saw that she was very depressed and had very less hope in her eyes about her future. Her husband and her mother were her constant support. We had a very difficult time motivating her.

It took almost six months for her to recover. During the first few weeks of her recovery time, the outcome of her progress was very poor and she started rejecting her life. She used to say that her life in the wheelchair was worthless and that death is better than continuing with the life she had. But I constantly tried to make her understand that her life is so important for her loved ones i,e. her parents, sister, and husband. Once it hit her mind she started giving good outcomes for my rehabilitation program. By the end of six months, she started walking with elbow clutches. Then she left for Sri Lanka.

After around 2 years suddenly one day she came back to meet me with a beautiful baby girl in her hand. She was still limping but walking on her own. I was so happy to see her leading a happy family life. But what she told me was a very great lesson for me. She told me that her rehabilitation experience helped her to overcome her physical disability to a certain extent but what really pushed her further was motivational talks and empathy to overcome the hurdles and maximize her progress.

My holistic approach with her and the "you can do it" mantra really helped her to train her body and mind and activated her extra potential stimulation which helped her to overcome the situation she was in. That day made me realize that even a doctor needs to go a little out of the way to get good results through training both the body and mind and through stimulating the extra potential ability that is there in every individual.

Through this story, I want to convey that if a person like Sura can overcome her physical disabilities and achieve the fitness goal through TYBM then an average person with less or no physical disability can do wonders by training the mind and activating the extra potential.

Why We Should Take Exercise Seriously

A good example of a human being is someone who is at their optimal weight and can keep it there without much effort because they are physically healthy. The prevention of many illnesses and health issues is another benefit of moving frequently. In addition to lowering the prevalence of illnesses like heart disease and weight, fitness has a positive effect on the muscle system, helping to grow and improve it.

"Take care of the body, it is the only precious treasure you own."

The Fitness Foundation

The two words **FITNESS FOUNDATION** is the fundamentals of employing the body effectively. The basis of your fitness is your capacity to carry out the activities of daily living at a level that is satisfactory for you and your work requirements. There's a yearly trend toward skipping the fundamentals in favor of a rigorous fitness regimen. Despite the obvious simplicity of these ideas, we appear to have lost how to implement them. If you don't have a firm grasp on these biochemical basics, you'll never be able to master your body and achieve your fitness objectives.

To be physically fit, one must be able to perform a wide range of common tasks without tiring out. I'll explain how:

Beginning today, you will devote your attention to the four foundational skills that must be learned in order to maximize the benefits of your physical activity.

- Breathing
- Rest, Fluid Intake, and Other Variables
- Competence in Postural Moving
- Strategies for Developing Your Workout

Though they're actually quite simple in nature, it will require some time and effort to incorporate them into a regular habit. None of these things probably come to mind when you think of "exercise," but keep in mind that exercise is a stimulation that elicits a bodily reaction.

As life span rises quicker than the proportion of that life spent in good health, known as "healthy life years," there are unexpected and significant societal, economic, and health issues that come along with it. Older individuals care less about being healthier and more about maintaining their current level of health and abilities. Hence it is important for every individual to train the body and mind in order to achieve physical fitness.

> *"The body achieves what the mind believes."*

There is one more story that I want to share to remind you all of the importance of willpower and the need to push your extra potential to fulfill your dreams of staying healthy. This is a real-life story that I cherish.

During my early phase of practice, I have seen lots of patients undergoing amputations. In India back then train accidents were the major cause of amputation. We used to rehabilitate these patients right from the very first stage of amputation, their prosthetic fittings and ambulation, walking, and back to functional activities of day-to-day living.

But as I was in the initial days of my profession I was not able to understand how some patients could easily overcome their disabilities to the fullest and would start leading a normal life than some patients who used to be depressed all the time and would blame the god and themselves for the situation they were in.

Now after many years of practice, I have realized that training the body and mind (TYBM) and extra potential stimulation (EPS) are the main role players in the life of physically challenged patients. I have seen many patients accepting their condition as the fate of bad luck and sulking over it and not doing anything much to improve their condition. But on the contrary, I have also come across patients with strong willpower and working hard by actively taking part in the rehabilitation program in order to live a normal life.

It's about a young girl, Neena, who was in her early thirties when she had both of her legs amputated at hip level.

Neena was always forced to wear a saree every day by her in-laws as a tradition. In the month of June, she draped a Nylon saree as the material would take less time to dry in the monsoon season. On that day she had to travel by train from Dombivali, Mumbai. Unfortunately, by the time she reached the platform, the train started moving and she planned to board the moving train, due to her bad luck she lost her balance while stepping in and her saree got stuck to the doors of the train and she fell under the moving train.

However, the people pulled her up and she was taken to the hospital, but by the time she became conscious her both legs were amputated from the hips. The same day when she left home she was 5.5 ft tall and in the evening she was only 3 ft in height. Such an unfortunate day it was for Neena.

Next, she was advised for rehabilitation and when I saw her for the first time she was almost in a depressed phase of her life. Her dreams were all shattered right in front of her eyes. Her own son who was 4 years old could not recognize her well.

However, as days passed, she was transformed from a depressed phase of life to a fully rehabilitated lady walking with prosthetics crutches. Her entire journey was amazing. I once asked her what was her ultimate dream and she said that she wanted to visit Kashmir with her son and family and wanted to go back to her teaching job. I must say she did achieve both of her dreams and it was possible only with her EPS and great family support. Her husband stood like a rock next to her and her in-laws supported her to the fullest.

That day made me realize that even with the disability she could reach her maximum potential because she focused on that extra

> potential she already had and the trust she kept in her family members. With this story, it is evident that fitness training and mind control can do wonders for a person's body.
>
> When such miracles are happening due to physical fitness and EPS, what are you, as a normal individual waiting for !

Pillars of Fitness Foundation

A strong foundation and sturdy pillars are necessary for any structure's durability and longevity. Similarly, if you want to live a long and fulfilling existence and put off premature aging and disability as much as possible, you should make exercise a regular part of your routine and adhere to the fitness core principles. Let's learn about the six pillars of a healthy exercise program.

1. Stamina or Cardiovascular Endurance
2. Flexibility/ mobility
3. Stretching
4. Muscle strength
5. Muscle endurance
6. Nutrition

In order to achieve these fitness pillars TYBM and EPS is very much essential. After going through each of the pillars you should allow your body to rest and recover only then your body will listen to your mind. However, achieving the first five pillars will only be possible if you feed your body well with nutritious food which is the last pillar known as nutrition. Unless your food intake is healthy you cannot even start with the first pillar. Hence, nutrition is one of the crucial parts of your fitness journey. Now you might be thinking what is the use of all the above pillars?

Once you start practicing all the pillars you will develop the right mental health and attitude.

For better understanding, I have given a pictorial representation of the pillars of fitness below.

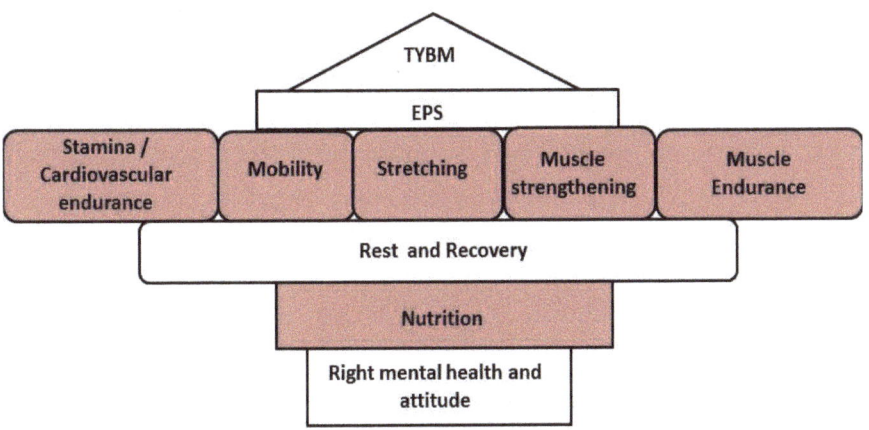

Fig 5.1: **Representation of the six pillars of fitness**

1. Cardiovascular Endurance/ Stamina

Cardiovascular endurance refers to a person's ability to perform whole-body aerobic activities at a modest to high effort for a prolonged period of time. Boosting your cardio stamina can give you more energy and help you get through the day. Diseases like diabetes, heart disease, and stroke are some of the risks that can be mitigated by this. In general, it can strengthen your endurance.

A Quick Summary of Aerobic Exercise

Aerobic exercise refers to low- to high-intensity physical activity in which oxygen-based aerobic metabolism is the primary means of energy production. It is the type of physical exertion that makes use of oxygen in order to meet the body's energy needs.

Advantages of Cardiovascular Endurance

You can improve your strength and fitness by engaging in physical activity and raising your heart rate. Many illnesses, including heart disease, obesity, Type 2 diabetes, cancer, and others, can be prevented through regular aerobic exercise. Some of the other advantages are

- **Better strength and stamina:** Your heart and lungs will strengthen as you exercise, giving you more strength and stamina. You will strengthen your muscles and bones. You may feel fatigued at first, but as you exercise regularly, your stamina will increase.
- **Balanced weight:** Maintaining a healthy weight can be accomplished through a combination of balanced food and regular aerobic activity.
- **Stronger bones:** Bone density increases with weight-bearing cardiovascular activity like strolling, which also helps lower the chance of osteoporosis.
- **Reducing dependence:** Strength training can help you maintain your mobility and independence for an extended period of time. You'll be less likely to hurt yourself tripping over something, too. Maintaining your fitness level enhances your quality of life as you get older.

You are now aware of how important it is to improve your aerobic stamina. The problem, however, is figuring out where to begin. Will you sign up for a fitness program just because your next-door friend did? Or are you going to start working out on your own without any prior planning? Which method will you use to kick off your daily regimen?

In any case, these are the sorts of inquiries that can naturally emerge for anyone. Here then, is the answer.

Keep It Simple

Get the basics down first. Just 15 minutes of exercise a day can have positive effects, especially for beginners. Try to get up to 30 minutes, three times a week. In eight to twelve weeks, you should noticeably increase your cardiovascular endurance if you follow this plan.

Exercise What You Love

Get involved in something you truly appreciate. The term "aerobic exercise" refers to any activity that requires you to use your large muscle groups and puts a greater demand on your cardiovascular system.

Know Your Limits

Put a limit on your efforts. Injuries are more likely to occur if you perform the same workout more than five times per week.

Go Slow

Build your way up slowly. The goal should be to increase the intensity of your activity by a small amount. Increase your speed or distance by no more than 10–20% per week. Exercise for 10 minutes at a time, and every week add 1 to 2 more minutes.

Warm, Stretch, and Relax

Get warmed up by exercising at a moderate intensity for 5-10 minutes. Gradually increase your workload until you reach your maximum effort.

However, once you start your cardio training it is important to know about your target heart rate. Target heart rate (THR) refers to the heart rate at which you want to exercise in order to maximize fitness benefits. Listed below is a formula you can use to figure it out by yourself.

Do it yourself

Depending on your exercise level, your target heart rate (THR) should be anywhere from 50 to 80% of your MHR. Maximum heart rate is calculated by subtracting your age from 220; for someone 45 years old, this yields a maximum heart rate of 175 (220- 45=175)

This is the utmost rate at which your pulse should pump per minute while you work out. For beginners, a heart rate of 50-60% (or 95-114 mph) is ideal. If you are at an advanced level then you will see a rise in your heart rate to around 170 beats per minute (80-90 percent of the maximum).

Tip: If you're just starting out in fitness, hiring a trainer can help you build aerobic stamina, understand your body's movement patterns, and nourish it properly.

2. Flexibility/Mobility

Flexibility is the absence of discomfort and restriction in movement across a specific range of motion, involving one or more joints and the accompanying muscle groups. Finding ways to be more adaptable will boost your quality of life in the long term and bring a host of advantages.

Benefits

Everyone, but particularly older people, need to be able to move freely and easily, so flexibility is not just a quality designated for sports. Mobility in old age, muscular healing, and a lower chance of harm are just a few of the many advantages.

When to Stretch

To get the most out of your flexibility routine, you should do it when your muscles are warm enough to extend further without discomfort. Warm up your muscles with a few minutes of light strolling before engaging in any stretching activities.

How much stretching will I need?

In general, you should repeat each stretching move three to five times during a single practice. In order to avoid injury, you should always ease into the intended posture gradually or whatever makes you feel most at ease. Hold the stretch for about 10 seconds if you haven't been doing it regularly. Regular stretching will make it less of a struggle. Over time, you'll improve to the point where you can easily maintain each exercise for 30 seconds.

Different Flexibility types

The two forms of flexibility are active and passive. The following chart summarizes the two primary categories of active flexibility: static and dynamic.

Table 5.1 Active flexibility and passive flexibility

	Active Flexibility		Passive Flexibility
Types	<ul><li>Ability to hold or pull your body into its maximum range of motion.</li><li>Active flexibility builds strength while also increasing range of motion.</li></ul>		<ul><li>Ability to hold or pull your body into its maximum range of motion with the help of a partner or of external help.</li></ul>
	Static	**Dynamic**	
	The full range of motion that can be achieved without movement.	The ability of the muscles and joints to move through a full range of motion during activities. It increases performance while decreasing the risk of injury	

3. Stretching

You might associate stretching with athletes like joggers and dancers. However, regular stretching is necessary for everyone to maintain their mobility without restriction. Many individuals are unaware of the importance of routine stretching.

Why should I stretch?

Flexibility in the muscles and joints is essential for health and mobility, and this can be achieved through regular stretching. The absence of this causes muscular shortening and stiffness. Tight hamstrings are a common symptom of prolonged sedentary behavior. It may become difficult to fully stretch the limb or bend the knee, limiting mobility and making it difficult to move. Similarly, if tense muscles are abruptly asked to perform a highly stretching activity, like playing tennis, they risk injury.

Fundamentals of Stretching

Make sure you know what you're doing with stretching so you can do it properly and securely before diving in. While stretching can be done pretty much anywhere, the method you use makes all the difference. If you stretch improperly, you could cause yourself more damage than benefit.

Follow these guidelines to avoid injury while stretching!

Remember that stretching is not a warmup: Exercising rigid, cold muscles can cause serious injury. Walking, running, or bicycling at a moderate effort for 5 to 10 minutes is a good warm-up before stretching.

Spend your time working the big muscles: Pay special attention to your legs, quadriceps, hips, lower back, neck, and shoulders as you extend.

Avoid bouncing: Lengthen with a gentle, non-bouncing motion. If you want to prevent muscular injury and increase flexibility, avoid bouncing as you stretch.

Hold your position: Maintain a natural breathing pattern while holding each stretch for 30–60 seconds, depending on the area(s) of concern. Stop trying to hurt yourself. When you extend, you should sense strain, but not pain. You've gone too far if you're experiencing pain.

Stay diligent with your stretches: Maintaining a regular stretching routine can take some effort. However, you will reap the greatest rewards if you exercise on a consistent basis (at least twice or thrice weekly). Practicing regular stretching for as little as 5 to 10 minutes can have positive effects.

Caution

Some people with injuries or persistent health issues may need to modify their exercise routines. Consider that extending an already stressed muscle could aggravate the injury. If you are concerned about your health, you should consult a doctor or physical trainer about the best method to exercise.

---

4. Muscle Strengthening

Muscle-strengthening exercise, also known as strength/ weight/ resistance training or exercise, is a form of physical activity that involves the voluntary use of external resistance, such as that provided by weight machines, exercise bands, hand-held weights, or one's own body weight (through, say, push-ups or sit-ups). Clinical exercise studies indicate that strength training leads to gains in skeletal muscular strength, power, stamina, and mass when practiced consistently.

How often should I do muscle-strengthening exercises?

- Ideally, you would spend two or more days a week engaging in muscle-strengthening activities that target all of your major muscle groups (the legs, hips, back, abdomen, chest, shoulders, and arms).
- It is not recommended that you train for a set amount of time, but a typical session may last less than 20 minutes.
- You should push yourself during exercises until you genuinely can't manage to do another repetition without assistance.
- One complete motion of an activity, such as lifting a weight or performing one push-up or one sit-up, is one repetition.
- One set consists of eight to twelve repetitions of an exercise. Doing muscle-strengthening exercises in at least two sets is beneficial, but doing three sets is optimal.
- Don't rush things; ease into it and work your way up over several weeks.

What kind of exercises should I do?

- Lifting weights
- Perform Exercises Using Resistance Bands

- Working in the garden that requires a lot of excavating and stooping
- Climbing Hills
- Cycling
- Squats, planks, and push-ups

However, people with a busy routine can start with a combination of exercises and strengthen their muscles.

5. Muscle Endurance

Muscle endurance is the length of time that a person's muscles can be worked without fatigue. Building up your muscle stamina is a great way to boost your health and fitness. Muscle density can be increased by elderly citizens aged 60 and up with the help of frequent physical workouts. For elderly people, keeping their muscles strong should be a top priority. The ability to do simple tasks like moving in and out of a recliner or bed, walking up and down steps, entering and exiting a vehicle, hauling heavy loads like washing or shopping, lifting up a youngster, or even using the restroom can be compromised by a loss of muscular power (3)

Benefits of Muscular Endurance Training

- Endurance exercise helps older adults gain muscle and enhance their breathing and cardiovascular systems.
- The muscles, circulatory system, bones, ligaments, and airways all benefit, allowing them to move and operate more efficiently.
- Help keep one's balance and posture in check for extended amounts of time

- Elevating Muscle Aerobic Capacity
- Enhancing Capabilities for Everyday Use Including Heavy Lifting

What type of endurance exercise should I do?

Pushups, squats, crunches, lunges and planks, water aerobics, brisk walking, and resistance exercises are some of the exercises that can be done by the elderly as well.

6. Nutrition

"Choices you make today keep you healthier tomorrow."

It's essential to keep up a healthy routine at any age, but it's particularly crucial for the elderly.

Seniors should drink plenty of water and consume a healthy diet to ensure optimal health. Maintaining a healthy body requires both a wholesome diet and regular activity. Your requirements shift as you get older. Follow these instructions to acquire the resources you need at this time in your life.

Eat Well!

- **Increase your calcium**: Eat dark green, leafy vegetables, canned fish, fortified cereal, milk, and fortified fruit juices.
- **Get more fiber**: Eat more fruits and vegetables.
- **Consume more protein:** Eat low-fat milk, meat, fish, poultry, and cooked or dried beans.
- **Reduce intake of salt**

- **Go for healthy fats:** Have nuts, seeds, fish, olive oil, and avocados.
- **Take more potassium:** Eat fruits, vegetables, and beans.
- **Take up the Mediterranean diet**: Eat a diet rich in fruit, vegetables, fish, whole grains, good fats, and low-fat dairy products.
- **Remember the beverages**: You may feel less thirsty as you age, so you may need to pay more attention to drinking enough liquids every day.
- Getting enough nutrition into your body while you work out is just as crucial as anything else.
- Please remember workouts and rest go hand in hand. Rest is as important as exercise and nutrition as you age. Above everything, a good mental attitude towards your life is very crucial. To keep your mind healthy and active never forget TYBM and EPS.

"Healthy food makes you feel good."

Now that I have explained the fitness foundation pillars, it's time for you to incorporate them into your daily routine. I hope the charts below will help you better grasp the various forms of physical exercise that can be pursued.

Due to the busy nature of modern life, it is not always feasible to exercise every day. If this is the case, you may find that combining different forms of exercise is the most effective. If you do exercises that target multiple muscles at once, you can get a full-body workout done in as little as 20 or 30 minutes. The following are a few instances of such a combo exercise.

Table 5.2 Exercises for various body parts

Body Parts	Exercise
Abdomen	Sit-ups + leg raises
Quads	Lunges + High knees
Glutes	Squats + Side leg raise
Tricep	Push up + Tricep dips
Bicep	Leg curls + Sitting pullups
Shoulders	Superman pose + Alternate arm and leg plank
Chest	Chest squeeze + Shoulder tap

There is another type of training of highly intense workouts in a short span of time which is known as HIIT.

The only difference between combination exercise and HIIT workouts is the intensity of the exercise.

High-intensity interval training is commonly referred to as HIIT. (HIIT). High-intensity interval training (HIIT) is superior to other forms of cardio for fat loss. Interval training entails going through periods of intense exercise (like jogging at 90 percent of your maximum heart rate) interspersed with periods of less intense exercise (like strolling at a modest speed) or relaxation. Do the exercise that is appropriate for your talent level, whether that be novice, middle, or expert. If you want to get in good exercise, give each movement 30 seconds of your time and 30 seconds of rest for as long as it takes.

1. Beginner (10-15 minutes)

2. Intermediate (20 minutes)
3. Advanced (30 minutes)

Table 5.3: HIIT workout chart for 25 - 30 mins

No. of Weeks	Warm up exercise	High-Intensity workout	Moderate intensity workout	Repetitions	Rest
1 – 2	↑ 5min ↓	Jumping jacks/Sprint (20 to 30 sec)	Jogging (5min)	↑ 4 times ↓	↑ 5 mins ↑
3 – 4		Jumping jacks/Sprint (30 to 45 sec)	Running (3min)		
5 – 6		Running at your own pace (45 to 60 sec)	Jogging at a slower pace (4mins)		

High-intensity interval training (HIIT) is a complex exercise method that necessitates instruction and supervision from a trained professional. If you are over the age of 40 and can exercise for 20 minutes at 70% to 90% of your maximal heart rate, a stress test is recommended to rule out any preexisting cardiac issues.

Boot Camp

High-intensity interval training (HIIT) is the foundation of a boot camp exercise, which consists of periods of rigorous action interspersed with periods of rest. Exercises that target multiple muscle groups and joints, like those performed in a boot camp, help improve daily fitness. Workouts at a boot camp combine aerobic, weight training, and sprint work into a single practice. The intense cardio and strength training of a boot camp is great for losing weight and getting in shape. In limited circumstances, this is a great way to get decent exercise. Do it at home! Here is a schedule of routines for boot camp exercises.

Table 5.4: Boot camp exercises

Exercise Type	Duration	Body Parts
Jumping jack	30 seconds	Full body workout + cardio
Squat	30 seconds	Glutes+ hamstrings+quads
Pushups	30 seconds	upper back, deltoids, triceps, chest, biceps
Jump rope	30 seconds	Full body workout + Cardio
Walking plank	30 seconds	full-body; arms+ core+ legs
Wall sits	30 seconds	glutes+quads+core
Mountain climber	30 seconds	full-body; arms+ core+legs

However, you should also be conscious of some details about cardiovascular health alongside the activities themselves. Aerobic exercise, or cardio for short, is any type of repetitive action that gets your heart rate up into the healthy range for sustained periods of time. Here is where you'll see the greatest fat and calorie loss.

Important acts about Cardio

Between 20% and 40% of a person's cardiac capacity is determined by genetics.

Maintain a constant awareness of your Max Heart Rate (MHR).

The time spent working out matters a great deal. At least 75 minutes of vigorous activity per week or 150 minutes of mild activity can be done.

Exercise, particularly mild to high-level exercise, improves sleep quality.

Excessive aerobic training is counterproductive. Keep it sensible, as there is a moment of declining results. (3 to 6 days per week, depending on your fitness level)

Just like other, more conventional forms of exercise, dancing is a great and enjoyable way to boost physical health.

Consider your level of ease, the intensity of your respiration, and the quantity of perspiration you believe you're producing while working out.

Don't hit your workouts on an empty stomach. If you fall short of energy during the workout then your body will start burning the muscles and not the fat

Split your exercise time into two or three 10- to 15-minute sessions daily.

You can enhance your health and well-being in countless ways by engaging in aerobic activities.

Not to forget the key rule for a healthy life is **consistency** which is the cornerstone to success.

TABATA

Tabata is a form of HIIT characterized by timed intervals of intense exercise followed by brief times of rest. Dr. Izumi Tabata, a Japanese speed skating instructor, is credited with creating the 4-minute, high-intensity exercise that has been shown to improve aerobic endurance and muscular power. You'll work hard for 20 seconds, then relax for 10 seconds, for a total of 4 minutes and this sequence will be repeated 8 times. (20 s X 8 rounds + 10s rest = 4 minutes) A full-body, high-intensity exercise can be completed in just 4 minutes. This whole process can be done for another 15–20 minutes.

Table 5.5: TABATA workout plan

High knees	Squats or lunges	Crunches	push-ups	Burpees
20 seconds at high intensity + 10 seconds of rest + 8 rounds = Total of 4 minutes				

> **Caution:**
>
> TABATA and HIIT are not for everyone. In order to participate in HIIT training, one must first complete a fitness progression that involves mild-intensity exercise, followed by muscular building with weights. When you have established a routine with HIIT exercises, you are ready to move on to the TABATA schedule. However, it is essential to consult a doctor or fitness trainer to rule out any underlying health conditions before beginning a new exercise routine. In this manner, you can avoid injury while getting the most out of your exercise.

The FIIT principle

Strength training suggestions often include the FITT Principle, but cardio (aerobic) exercise and weight reduction are its primary applications. The FITT concept can be used by anyone, from exercise newbies to seasoned athletes. FITT stands for:

- frequency
- intensity
- time
- type

The FIIT concept consists of several interrelated parts, all of which work together to get you in shape. It works wonderfully as a tool for tracking the results of both aerobic and weight training sessions.

Table 5.6: FIIT table

	Aerobic/ Cardio	Flexibility	Muscular Endurance	Muscular Strength	Balance
Frequency	3-5 times a week	Daily warm up and cool down	Daily for some muscle group	3 times a week, different muscle groups	3 to 5 times a week
Intensity	60 - 90 % of maximum heart rate	Hold for 15 - 30 secs, 1-3 reps	15 rep, 8 to 12 exercise	70 to 90 % of 1 rep max.	Hold for 30 sec. 3 reps alternately left and right foot.
Time	15 - 60 min Continous activity	15 - 20 mins	30 - 60 mins Progressive	15 - 60 min Progressive	5 min rest after each interval
Type of exercise	Zumba, Running or Cycling	Static stretch/Dynamic stretch	Resistance training, Body weight, circuit training	Resistance training	One leg stand

Sequence of exercise

One statement sums up the correct workout sequence for most individuals, most of the time which is the following:

More demanding exercises should be performed before less demanding exercises.

Here are the most common examples of what the above statement means:

1. **Exercises targeting larger muscles should be performed before those targeting smaller muscles.**

    Examples: Chest or back before shoulders, biceps, or triceps; shoulders before biceps or triceps; quads or hamstrings before calves or abs

2. **It's best to perform compound movements first, followed by solo exercises.**

    Examples: Bench press before dumbbell flyes; overhead press before lateral raises; squats before leg extensions; Romanian deadlifts before leg curls

3. **The use of free weights and body weight should precede the use of workout equipment.**

    Examples: Squats or deadlifts before leg presses; barbell bench press before incline machine press; pull-ups before chest-supported machine rows

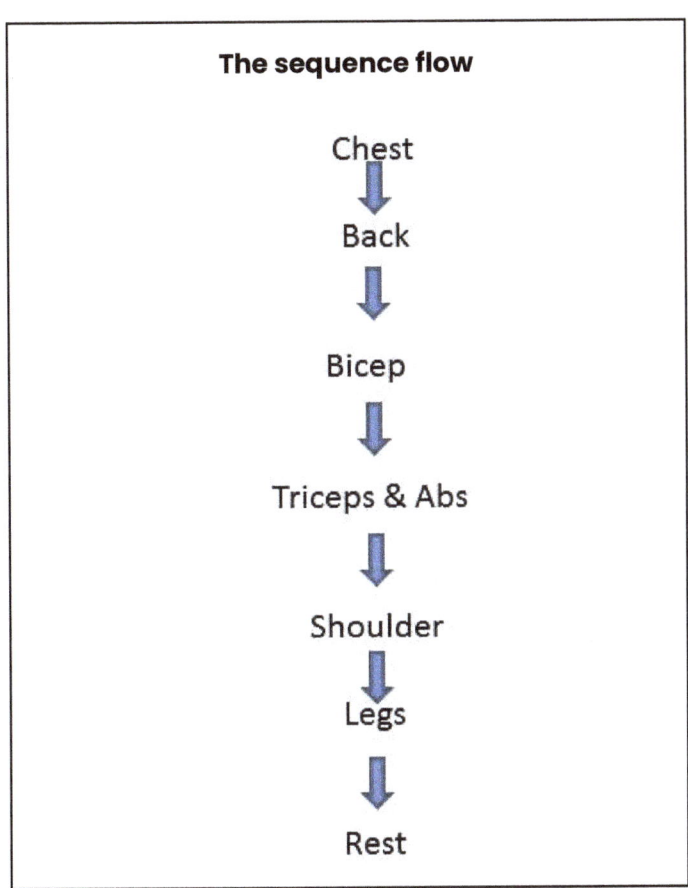

Fig 5.1 Sequence of Exercise

How do we find out the intensity of weight training?

Now that we know about the sequence of exercise it is equally important to know how strenuous (or light) are your workouts. Getting the most out of your workout requires striking a balance between pressing yourself too hard and not pushing yourself hard enough. Learn more about the concept of exercise intensity and how to get the most out of your next practice here.

Choosing Your Exercise Intensity

Aerobic Activity: Perform at least 75 minutes of intense aerobic exercise per week, such as jogging or aerobic dancing, or 150 minutes of mild aerobic activity, such as fast strolling, swimming, or mowing the grass.

Strength Training: Train your muscles by lifting weights at least twice a week. Exercises that utilize either loose weights, weight equipment, or the individual's own body weight should be considered. You can also do squats, splits, and lunges. One series of each exercise should be performed, with weight or force increased until muscular fatigue occurs after 12–15 rounds.

In order to reap the greatest health benefits from exercise, your workouts should typically be mild-to-intense in terms of the effort. If you're just getting started with working out, ease into it. Gradually work up to a comfortable level of effort.

Think about why you want to work out. Is your goal to get in better shape, shed some pounds, improve your competitive skills, or do all of the above? Keep your expectations in check and don't overextend yourself. If you have any health concerns or are unsure of how vigorously you should exercise, consult your doctor. Below I have provided a workout schedule for your understanding.

Table 5.7: Workout Schedule

Monday	30-Minute Cardio Medley Workout + Upper Body Training + Stretch
Tuesday	30-Minute Treadmill Interval Workout + Core Training + Stretch
Wednesday	Low Impact Cardio Blast Workout (two circuits) + Lower body strength + Lower body stretch
Thursday	Rest or gentle yoga/stretching
Friday	Total Body Strength or Circuit Training
Saturday	Cardio Endurance Workout
Sunday	Rest

Rate of Perceived Exertion

In order to accurately calculate or feel the intensity of your workout I am providing a reference scale known as Borgs scale. The severity of a workout can be gauged using the Borg Rating of Perceived Exertion (RPE). How hard you think your body is working is known as perceived effort. It relies on the physiological changes a person notices in response to exercise, such as a faster heart rate, deeper breaths, more perspiration, and greater muscular exhaustion. Use the Borg Scale to rate your exertional discomfort. By keeping track of the extent to which your body is working, you can make necessary adjustments to the activity, such as increasing or decreasing the pace.

Borg's Scale

Table 5.8: Borg's Scale

Scale	Talk Test	Type of Activity/Exercise
0	Normal breathing	Relaxing
1	Normal breathing and can talk normally	Daily activities besides sleeping
2	Normal breathing and can talk normally	Walking
3	Light breathing, can carry a conversation	Light jogging
4	Moderate breathing	Fast walk or jog
5	Heavy breathing, still can carry on a conversation	Very fast walking and jog
6	Heavier breathing, can talk one to two sentences	Running
7	Broken sentences, heavy breathing	Fast running
8	Very heavy breathing, can say a word or two	Running much faster
9	Race pace	Can't talk, very heavy breathing
10	Race pace to win	Can't talk, Grasping for breath

Do it yourself!

You can evaluate your cardiovascular ability, muscle strength and stamina, flexibility, and body fat percentage, among others, without leaving the comfort of your own house using a variety of tests that are analogous to the Borg's scale. Thus below I have provided a chart using which you can measure your strength and endurance to gauge your fitness level. The below chart is for partial sit-ups. Record the maximum number you were able to do properly, at an adequate speed, then refer to the results interpretation table to determine the category you fall into.

Women

Table 5.9: Chart for Women

Age	15 - 19	20 - 29	30 -39	40 - 49	50 - 59	60 -69
Excellent	25	25	25	25	25	25
Very good	22-24	18-24	19-24	19-24	19-24	17-24
Good	17-21	14-17	10-18	11-18	10-18	8-16
Fair	12-16	5-3	6-9	4-10	6-9	3-7
Needs Improvement	<or=11	<or=4	<or=5	<or=3	<or=5	<or=2

Men

Table 5.10: Chart for Men

Age	15 - 19	20 - 29	30 -39	40 - 49	50 - 59	60 -69
Excellent	25	25	25	25	25	>or=25
Very good	23-24	21-24	18-24	18-24	17-24	16-24
Good	21-2	16-20	15-17	13-17	11-16	11-15
Fair	16-20	11-15	11-14	6-12	8-10	6-10
Needs Improvement	<or=15	<or=10	<or=10	<or=5	<or=7	<or=5

Circuit Training

Circuit training is a type of exercise in which you shift quickly between sets of movements (typically five to ten) that target various muscle areas. As a result, you get a full-body exercise that challenges your aerobic and muscle stamina. When you do circuit exercise, you won't have time to get tired. This is a cardiovascular and strength-training exercise in one. You'll be rotating rapidly between eight to ten workout machines designed to target specific muscle areas. Without spending any time, the necessary amount of rounds are finished in cycles. Below is an example of a core body circuit workout

3 circuits | 3 exercises | 3 rounds

Table 5.11: Circuit Training

Circuit 1	Circuit 2	Circuit 3
30 alternate toe touch crunch	30s x rotating mountain climber	30s x crunch
30 feet off crunch	30s x alternate leg raises	30s x full plank
30 alternate superman	30s x bow pose activation	30s x leg raise side to side
1 min rest		

The 3-Minute Stretch

Stretching is an essential part of a fitness program. Many people skip this because they can't work it into their already packed schedules. The good news is that even a brief stretching practice can help, even if it's only a few minutes first things in the morning. "One of the best methods to improve your health is to make stretching a regular part of your early practice. "No matter how you slept, the Daily Essential Three-Minute Sequence will give you a natural boost of vitality that will last longer than a cup of coffee. I have mentioned a few stretching postures for your reference.

1. Foot and hand stretch
2. Forearm stretch
3. Chest stretch
4. Spinal twist
5. Backstretch

6. Neck stretch
7. Glute stretch
8. Quad stretch
9. Hamstring and low backstretch
10. Chest and side stretch

Minor Pillars of Fitness/ Skill Components

Before I conclude I need to mention the Six minor pillars of fitness which are even more vital than the major pillars. They are:

Speed, Power, Agility, Reaction Time, Reflexes, and Coordination

A person's performance in physical exercise is influenced by a number of skill components/minor foundations. The speed and precision with which one can alter direction. The mastery of one's physical movements while still or in motion. The use of one's eyes and other senses to coordinate a physical action. The rapidity of motion, either of the whole body or of particular regions. Example: The 100-meter sprint of a track competitor rapid bat movement preceding a successful baseball strike

The capacity to carry out an action with power and swiftness. A volleyball competitor spiking the ball while aloft. Possession of lightning-fast reflexes in response to sensory input (a stimulus). Someone who sprints from the starting blocks at the sound of the cannon during a track contest.

A person's performance in athletics and other types of physical exercise is influenced by a variety of skill factors. Components of competence aid in illness prevention and raise the standard of living for individuals. Agility is the fast and effortless ability to alter one's direction of movement and bodily posture. Coordination, reflex, balance, speed, and the ability to adapt to a constantly shifting environment are all necessary skills.

Hence, it is of utmost importance to incorporate both major pillars and minor pillars of fitness foundation throughout your journey of a healthy life.

Take-Home Messages

- Always plan your exercise routine.
- Do your regular exercise and follow the 6 pillars of fitness foundation to die young as late as possible.
- Remember, a strong building needs a strong foundation and strong pillars. Same way, imagine your body as a structure and take care of it by doing regular exercises.
- Every pillar of a fitness foundation has a benefit. Follow them and improve your healthy aging.
- Above all fuel up your body with good nutrition in order to stay young and healthy as you age.
- Do not forget that your body and health is the only wealth you have which nobody can take away from you. So, look after it.

Self- Assessment

- Have you planned your routine?
- Are you doing the daily activities that you love?
- Do you do cardio regularly?
- Have you measured your target heart rate?

- Did you consult the doctor before starting your fitness foundation exercises?
- Are you practicing TYBM and EPS?

CHAPTER 6

Joint Health Is the Only Way to be

Sitting is the new smoking emphasis on joint health.

A joint is a connection between two or more bones. The joints in your skull, for example, are rigid, while other joints in your body, such as your knees, hips, and shoulders, are mobile. Maintaining good joint health is essential if you want to engage in activities like running, walking, jumping, and playing sports. Maintaining your health and the health of your joints is possible via regular exercise, a nutritious diet, the avoidance of injuries, and enough rest.

Regardless of the health of the person, age-related alterations will eventually limit the range of motion in their joints. Reduced mobility in a joint may have serious consequences for how you stand and move. Disability and shorter life expectancy may be directly attributed to arthritis and joint discomfort. It's believed that 9 percent of people have discomfort in their shoulders, 7 percent in their hips, 7 percent in their fingers, and 18 percent in their knees. Because lubricating fluid within the joints declines and the cartilage thins with age, joint movement becomes stiffer and less flexible. Arthritis contributes to falls in one-third of those over 65 every year. It is estimated that half of all Americans will get knee osteoarthritis by the time they are 85.

Lack of exercise is a major contributor to the degenerative changes that occur in joints with age. The Centers for Disease Control and Prevention reports that the greater levels of estrogen in women make them more vulnerable to joint instability than males. In 2010, those between the ages of 45 and 64 accounted for 42% of all hip and knee replacement surgeries. Knee, foot, and hand osteoarthritis affects 27% of women aged 45 to 54.

> *"Keep your joints healthy, and stay young forever."*

"How healthy you are" is defined not by your age but by your joint mobility. Hence, I would like to share a small real-life story.

Ratna was a very rich lady in a town. She was just around 55 years old. But had no control over her food, health, and nutrition and she never performed any exercise in her lifetime. As a result, she developed all sorts of diseases at an early age such as diabetes, hypertension, and arthritis. Along with it she was overweight and had severe pain in her joints. After a year she became dependent on her movements. She had to take support to walk. One day Ratna was invited as a chief guest for a function to felicitate the young talent which was organized by her family. But as she was called on stage she felt very embarrassed because she was finding it very difficult to walk on her own and people had to help her to reach the stage. That for Ratna was a turning point in her life. From then on she challenged herself to improve her health condition. On her fitness journey and with all of our support as doctors and dieticians she lost significant weight and her joint health also improved tremendously. She also regained her confidence in life.

Hence, this story should remind you that taking small steps will lead to a big change in your health. A daily dose of little exercise will help you increase your health span and improve your quality of life.

Six Joints and One Spine

[Shoulder joints, Elbow joints, Wrist joints, Hip joints, Knee joints, and Ankle joints]

Articular cartilage is one of several tissues that make up a joint, along with the capsule, meniscus, and ligaments, and it serves a crucial role in ensuring the joint continues to function mechanically competently even when subjected to intense physical activity. Regular weight-bearing exercise has several advantages, one of which is increased circulation of blood and synovial fluid inside a joint.

It seems that today's youth spend too much time sitting. The elderly use sitting as an excuse to spend much of their day idling. But are you aware of how hazardous sitting is to your health? Perhaps you're wondering why sitting is such a poor idea. I've addressed your question below. Please read it!!

What are the major health risks associated with excessive sitting?

One of the main issues is that the discs between the lumbar vertebrae begin to bulge, which is a chronic condition. When a disc protrudes or even herniates, the surrounding muscles tighten to prevent any additional injury. It's good if we're not moving about, but our bodies weren't designed for it. When we attempt to get up and start moving around again, we are pushing our stiff muscles to do something they were not designed to do. Maintaining good joint health is essential if you want to engage in activities like running, walking, jumping, and playing sports.

Sitting for extended periods is bad for our health, but most of us are guilty of doing just that. People of all ages and professions spend much too much time seated in front of a screen. While research continuously demonstrates the drawbacks of a sedentary lifestyle. As sedentary work habits become the norm, people lose physical fitness and become more prone to joint injuries. Below, I have listed some common causes of joint pain.

Common Causes of Joint Pain

Table 6.1: Causes of joint pain

Arthritis	Inflammation that causes stiffness and pain in the joints (rheumatoid arthritis or gout) or degeneration (osteoarthritis)
Bursitis	Inflammation of the bursae (fluid-filled sacs that cushion and pad bones
Sprain	Tearing and stretching of ligaments
Tendonitis	Inflammation, irritation, and swelling of a tendon that is attached to the joint
Osteoarthritis (OA)	It is the most common form of arthritis in the world. It can be classified into 2 categories: primary osteoarthritis and secondary osteoarthritis.

	Classically, OA presents with joint pain and loss of function
Rheumatoid arthritis or RA	It is an autoimmune and inflammatory disease. RA commonly affects joints in the hands, wrists, and knees. In a joint with RA, the lining of the joint becomes inflamed, causing damage to joint tissue

Importance of Exercise

Everyone needs exercise. Regular exercise improves muscle strength and mobility. Joint discomfort is lessened and fatigue is fought off with regular exercise.

Of course, the concept of walking around the block or swimming a few laps may seem like too much when joints are tight and sore. Exercising at a low intensity might help you feel better and maintain a healthy weight. In a nutshell, exercise may keep you going even while arthritis attempts to slow you down.

Selective forms of exercise may boost fitness and health without causing unnecessary joint damage. Exercising as part of a therapy plan may improve health and well-being and it can:

- Strengthen muscles around joints
- Help maintain bone strength
- Increase energy
- Make it easier to sleep well
- Help control weight
- Improve balance
- Improve mood

Aim for at least 150 minutes per week of moderate-intensity aerobic activity. If it helps your joints to work out for just 10 minutes at a time, go for it.

Know Your Joints

As was previously discussed, a joint is a connection between two or more bones that allows for those bones to move. Except for the throat bone, every single bone in the body connects to another bone at a joint. A joint's function determines its shape.

Types of Joints

1. Shoulder Joints

Because it's a ball-and-socket joint, your shoulder can do a lot of different things. You need these muscles to do things like to toss a ball or reach for something on a high shelf. The shoulder joint allows for greater mobility than any other joint in the human body.

Diseases Associated with Shoulder Joints

Arthritis and bursitis are the prevalent issues that affect the shoulder joints.

Exercises to Protect the Shoulder Joint

Table 6.2: Exercises for shoulder joint

1.	Bicep curls	Will make lifting activities easier.
2.	Overhead elbow extension	Improves your ability to lift your arms above your shoulders when reaching high to a shelf.
3.	Triceps kickbacks	Improve your ability to rise from a chair, making reaching a high shelf easier.
4.	Diagonal inward shoulder raise	Increase the mobility of your shoulder for better arm swing while walking.
5.	Diagonal outward shoulder raise	Improve your shoulder mobility.
6.	Shoulder rolls	Improves mobility and stabilizes your shoulder blades for heavier lifting.
7.	Overhead press	Stabilizes the back muscles and shoulder and increases the mobility of the shoulder joint.

2. Elbow Joint

The elbow is the movable joint between the upper arm and the forearm. You put a lot of stress on your elbow joints every day. However, the elbow joint may become painfully injured from overuse or from being used excessively. The flexibility of the elbow allows for a full 180-degree range of motion, which is useful for lifting and carrying heavy loads. The elbow is essential for tugging, lifting, and even eating. Actions like throwing and stretching are made possible by the elbow joint as well.

Problems Associated with the Elbow Joint

Arthritis is a frequent source of elbow pain. Wear and tear from advancing age and routine usage, as well as injuries such as fractures and dislocations, are all potential causes of impairment. Arthritis in the elbow makes it uncomfortable to bend the arm, making everyday life difficult. If you know how to take care of your elbows and prevent injuries, you won't have to worry about elbow discomfort.

Hence, I am providing a list of exercises important to maintain the functioning of the elbow joint.

Table 6.3: Exercises for elbow joint

Exercise	Repetitions
Fist clench	10 secs; 10 rep
Supination with a dumbbell	20 times on each side
Towel twist	10 times in each direction
Wrist lift (palm up)	3 sets; 15 rep
Elbow bend	15 to 30 sec; 10 times
Bicep wall stretch	Hold for 60 secs; repeat 5 times

3. Wrist Joint

The wrist joints are located between the numerous bones that make up the wrist and forearm. This complicated joint connects the hand to the forearm. Through elevating, grasping, and rotating, the wrist enables the majority of our daily activities. Regardless of the substantial amount of physical demand, we frequently take our wrists for granted. Without sufficient mobility and strength, they are more susceptible to injury and discomfort. The wrist joints enable us to flex or extend our palms.

Problems with the Wrist Joint

Osteoarthritis of the Hand and Wrist

Joints in the fingers and wrists are particularly vulnerable in the aged population. Joint aging, reduced synovial fluid production, and cartilage thinning are the major causes of osteoarthritis in the hands and wrists. Stiffness, swelling, and discomfort in the wrist joint are all possible symptoms.

Exercises to Maintain the Wrist Joint Mobility

Table 6.4: Exercises of the wrist joint

Exercises	Repetitions/ Time
Kneeling forearm stretch	30 seconds
Sponge squeeze	10 seconds, 10 times
Wrist rotations	3 to 5 seconds, 10 times
Wrist circles	15 seconds, each hand
Clenched fists	Hold for 105 secs and repeat 10 times

4. Hip Joint

The hip joint is the point at which a thigh meets the upper part of the body. The joint has a ball-and-socket design. The hip is the point where the thigh bone and the pelvis connect. The femur is the bone in your thigh, while the hip is the bone in your pelvis.

What does it do?

- Ensures that your upper body is stable and supported
- Helps to bend your knee and thigh
- Maintains your weight

Problems Associated with Your Hip Joint

- **Osteoarthritis:** Inflammation of your joints that causes pain and swelling
- **Osteoporosis:** Bone weakness that may cause them to break easily
- **Hip dysplasia:** Your thigh bone doesn't fit together in your pelvis as expected
- **Bursitis:** Swelling of the fluid-filled sac in your joint

I have given a chart of exercises to maintain the flexibility of your hip joint.

Table 6.5: Exercises for hip joint

Exercises	Duration/Rep
Butterfly Pose	60 secs
Standing hip extension	30 to 60 secs, 10 times, repeat for each leg

Prone straight leg raise	3 secs, 5 times, repeat for each leg
Side hip raises	5 secs; 5 times
Hip marches	10 to 15 times on each side
Hip rotation	30 secs in each direction

5. Knee Joint

The knee is the hinge point where the bones of the lower leg and upper leg connect. The knee is the body's biggest joint, and its flexibility allows you to sit, stoop, walk, and even leap. It aids with standing, walking, and balancing.

Problems Associated with the Knees

- Arthritis
- Osteoarthritis
- Bursitis
- Tendinitis
- Osteoporosis

Below is a list of exercises to maintain knee joint stability:

Table 6.6: Exercises for knee joint

Exercises	Duration/Rep
Seated Knee extension	5 secs, 10 times
Squats with a chair	10 secs, 5 times
Hamstring curls standing	10 times, each leg

Quad sets	5 secs, 10 times
Straight leg raise	5 secs each leg, 5 times

6. Ankle Joint

The ankle is one of many joints in the lower leg. Leg bones (tibia and fibula) and foot bones come together to form them. Extreme pressure and stress are placed on the ankle joint. For example, when you run and leap, the forces acting on your ankles might be many times your body weight.

What does it do?

The ankle joint permits the foot to move in a vertical and lateral plane which is up and down and side-to-side movement.

Problems Associated with Ankle Joints

- Ankle arthritis
- Rheumatoid arthritis
- Gout
- Psoriatic arthritis

Here are some exercises that you need to do to maintain ankle joint strength:

Table 6.7: Exercises for ankle joint

Exercises	Duration/ Rep
Standing heel raises	10 times on each side
Single leg balance with rotation	2 rounds of 60 secs

Single-leg lateral Jumps	2 rounds of 60 secs
Towel stretches	30 secs, 3 times
Calf raise	times

Spine

The spine or backbone is a complex structure of small bones (vertebrae), cushioning disks, nerves, joints, ligaments, and muscles. It is your body's central support structure.

The spine joint, like all the others, is crucial to our everyday functioning. There are 24 vertebrae (spinal bones) in your spine, and 23 discs cushion the bones and keep them in place. The spinal discs cushion the spine, strengthen it, and allow it to bend and twist in all directions. There are a total of 364 joints in your spine. All those joints cooperate to bear your body weight, so you can go in all sorts of crazy ways and do crazy things.

For many elderly people, discomfort is brought on by the deterioration of spinal joints. Age-related degeneration of the spinal discs, joints, and other spinal structures, as well as nonspecific sources of pain such as muscular strain, are common in adults aged 50 and more, making them particularly susceptible to lower back pain.

The spine's joints are often referred to as Facet Joints. Its purpose is to help you stand up straight and move about easily. Three segments make up the spine joint: the cervical spine, the dorsal spine, and the lumbar spine.

Cervical Spine

Facet joints connect the neck to the rest of the spine. They let you move your head and neck in all directions. Strength, stamina, and mobility in the neck and shoulders are essential for good cervical spine posture.

Problems Associated with Cervical Spine

Wear and tear on the bones, discs, and joints of the neck over time leads to a disease called cervical osteoarthritis, often known as cervical spondylosis or arthritis in the neck. As we become older, the discs in our cervical spine dry up and tighten up.

Exercises to Maintain the Cervical Spine

Table 6.8: Exercises for cervical spine

Exercises	Rep/secs
Overhead arm reach	5 times; each side
Knee to chest	Hold 5 secs; repeat times
Thoracic extension	Hold for 5 secs and repeat 10 times
Reverse dumbbell	3 sets; 18-12 reps
Lateral raise	8 - 12 times/ set

Dorsal spine

This section of your spine, also known as the thoracic spine, connects the bottom of your neck to the bottom of your rib cage.

What does it do?

Your rib cage stabilizes your dorsal spine, and in turn, your dorsal spine stabilizes your rib cage. The rib cage and the vertebral column work together to protect vital organs such as the heart and lungs.

Maintaining a healthy range of motion in the dorsal spine is essential for regular activities. After all, we aren't mechanical beings programmed to go on a straight path. The dorsal spine allows you to bend and reach into cabinets, walk about in the yard, get out of the vehicles, and rise from beds.

Hence, to maintain the mobility of your dorsal spine. I have provided a list of exercises below.

Table 6.9: Exercises for dorsal spine

Exercises	Rep/duration
1. Pelvic tilt	
2. Knee hugs	
3. Knee rolls	
4. Shoulder bridge	
5. Supine rotation stretch	30 secs, 5 times
6. Child pose	
7. Roll downs	
8. Seated rotation	
9. Arm opening	

Lumbar Spine

The lumbar spine is located in the lower back and is made up of vertebrae, intervertebral discs, nerves, muscles, ligaments, and blood vessels.

What does it do?

- It helps keep your upper body in place and spreads your weight evenly.
- Your ability to move depends on the strength of your lower back muscles and the mobility of your lumbar spine.
- It makes sure your spinal cord is safe.
- It keeps your legs going strong.

Problems Associated with the Lumbar Spine

- Lower back pain
- **Lumbar stenosis:** Stenosis is a narrowing of the space around your spinal cord.
- **Spondylolisthesis:** This condition happens when a lumbar vertebra slips out of place.
- Sciatica
- Herniated disk
- Degenerative disk disease

Exercises to Maintain the Lumbar Spine Movement

Table 6.10: Exercises for lumbar spine

	Exercises	Duration/Rep
1.	Knee-to-chest stretch	30 to 60 secs, 5 times
2.	Piriformis stretch	30 to 60 secs, repeat 5 times with both legs
3.	Lower trunk rotation	30 to 60 secs, 5 times
4.	Hamstring stretch	30 to 60 secs, repeat 5 times with both legs

Everyone experiences aging differently. However, being in good health is a must for participating in many of these pursuits. The ability to move freely, feel energized, and look forward to the future all depend on a spine that is in excellent condition. Following these guidelines will help you maintain a healthy spine and back.

- Pay attention to your posture.
- Put on shoes that will give you support.
- Follow a healthy eating pattern.
- Strengthen your body with exercises.
- Maintain your flexibility.
- Calm your mind.

The health of your spine and six joints define your age. Thus, I am going to share a real incident to stress joint and spine health.

Rupa was one of my close friends for many years and I was her doctor and her well-wisher. Our children went to University at the same time. Rupa had neglected her health very badly. She was overweight. Her posture was very bad and her walk was very slow and slaying. Overall she aged very badly. One day she asked me a funny question and that took me by surprise. She said she visited her daughter and son in the US when they were in their first year at University. She wanted to spend a good time with her kids, but walking and her health was real problem. During her stay in the US, there was a meeting with the parents and professors along with the children in the University. But Rupa got to know about the gathering only when one of her friends asked her. Rupa was surprised as her children never invited her. The next evening, she asked her children about the gathering but her children did not speak a word. But after she insisted the daughter said that she was not comfortable introducing her mother to her friends and professor as Rupa had a bad posture and was not presentable like other fit parents. Rupa felt bad for what her children did. Her children were wrong for body shaming their mother but Rupa also should understand that her health and joints are a priority. But she took the incident sportively and gave a try to improve her health by losing weight and doing exercises.

So, the point I'm trying to make with this tale is that it's crucial to take care of your body, particularly your joints if you want to age gracefully and increase your health span.

Tips for a Healthy Joint!

1. Stay in motion: The golden rule of joint health is that the more you move, the less stiffness you'll have.
2. Shed some pounds: The hips, knees, and back all feel the effects of extra weight. Losing a little amount of weight may help.
3. Stretching: Better mobility may be achieved by regular stretching. Do your best to stretch three times a week, if not more often.
4. Flex some muscles: Increase your strength and muscle mass to reduce the strain on your joints. A little increase in force is noticeable.
5. Know your limits: Exercise-related muscular soreness is common, so be aware of your limits. But if you're still in pain after 48 hours, you could have overdone it.
6. Be mindful of your diet: If you suffer from rheumatoid arthritis-related joint discomfort, eating fish may provide some relief. Salmon and mackerel, two fatty cold-water fish, are rich in omega-3 fatty acids that are beneficial to joint health.
7. Strengthen your Bones: Vitamin D and calcium may be helpful. Green, leafy vegetables like broccoli and kale are also good providers of calcium, but dairy products are the best source.
8. Focus on your posture: Protect your neck, shoulders, hips, and knees by focusing on your posture. Your posture will benefit from going for a walk as well.
9. Lighten up: When lifting and carrying heavy objects, be mindful of your joints.

What exercises can be performed at home to keep joints mobile and pain-free is a question you may be asking yourself if you suffer from joint discomfort. So, here is a solution.

Crazy Joint Movements

This is one type of exercise where you randomly move your joints. You need not follow any particular workout plan to do this movement. Before you start your regular exercise you can first warm yourself by gently rubbing your body with a cotton cloth and then start with the joint movement. You can do this by randomly shaking your fingers first and then your entire hands till you feel the sensations in your shoulders. In a similar way, you can also make random movements in all of your six joints and then relax.

Another way of exercising your joints is by following mobility exercises. Just as you train for aerobic endurance, strength, and flexibility, you also need to train for mobility, especially if you want to maintain a vibrant, active life. Mobility refers to the way your joints move inside their socket. "Mobility is the ability to move your joints freely with the surrounding tissues allowing the movement to happen smoothly." Exercises to improve mobility tend to be more dynamic than exercises to improve flexibility. If you don't have flexibility or mobility, in time it can get harder to do simple things like getting in and out of your car, bending down to put on your shoes, or reaching up to get something out of a cupboard.

Thus, below I have provided you with a 7 days' workout plan to help you get more mobile. After two weeks of consistently doing each of the following exercises, you should begin to see positive results. You should immediately cease these activities if you experience any discomfort. People who already have injuries should not do these activities.

Table 6.11: Workout plan

Days	Exercises	Rep/ time
Day 1	Bicep curls	10 times (Switch arms)
	Lunges	3 sets of 5 reps with each leg
	Child's pose to downward-facing dog	3 times, taking three or more deep breaths
Day 2	Deep squat	Repeat 8 to12 times.
Day 3	Chest and shoulder opener	Repeat 8 to 12 times.
Day 4	Rest	
Day 5	Hamstring and hip opener	Repeat 8 to 12 times (Switch sides and repeat.)
Day 6	Arm and shoulder circles	Repeat 10 times for each side.
Day 7	Hip thrust	Repeat 10 to 12 times.

Self-Assessment

- Are you following the tips for a healthy joint?
- Do you do regular 7 days workouts for your joints?
- Have you decided to take a step forward to lose weight for the sake of joints?
- Are you aware of the minor pains that you may observe in your joints? If yes. Are you taking precautions for the same and consulting a doctor?
- Do you still sit for long hours?

Take-Home Messages

- Sitting is the new smoking. Hence avoid it as much as possible.
- Always plan a 7-day exercise routine and stay consistent for better results.
- Be aware of all your joints and their functioning.
- Try and do activities that will involve all of your six joints and spine.
- Always remember that lifestyle factors such as cigarette smoking, alcohol, and no physical activity can lead to joint problems such as arthritis. BEWARE OF IT!!!
- Do not ignore your health at any cost as health is the only wealth you have got throughout your life.

CHAPTER 7

Yoga – Way to Go

Embark on a journey to holistic well-being through ancient yoga.

Yoga is an ancient practice that aims to improve one's health on all levels: physical, mental, emotional, and spiritual. Between 2500 and 5000 years ago is when yoga first appeared. The Sanskrit word for yoga means "to unite," much like the yoke that links a chariot to its horses. The nontheistic integrative version of yoga known as *Raja Yoga* has eight limbs (*Astanga*) and is said to have been written about by the sage *Patanjali* (ca. 500 B.C.E.). The eight "limbs" of a tree are a common metaphor for the many components of yoga. general ethics (*Yama*), personal ethics (*niyama*), physical postures (*asana*), controlling one's breathing (*pranayama*), sensory withdrawal (*pratyahara*), focus (*dharana*), meditative (*dhyana*), and happiness (*samadhi*).

Yama, the first of the eight limbs, Yama refers to commitments, disciplines, or practices that focus on our relationship with the external world. The five yamas are *Ahimsa*, truthfulness (*Satya*), non-stealing (*Asteya*), non-violence (*Brahmacharya*), and non-covetousness (*Aparigraha*).

Niyama is the second of the eight limbs of yoga, and although it often relates to inward practices, it may also be interpreted in terms of how we interact with the environment. There are five practices known as the *Niyamas*, and they are *Saucha, Santosha, Tapas, Svadhyaya,* and *Isvarapranidaha.*

Asana, the third limb, is a solid and pleasant position that aids in achieving emotional and mental balance. The point of ergonomic seating is to alleviate physical discomfort and mental unrest, allowing us to focus on the task at hand without being 'pulled' away. No matter whether you're a yoga beginner or an experienced practitioner.

Pranayama is the cultivation of one's vital force or Prana. It may be used to define both the energy of the cosmos and the basic essence that sustains our lives. The breath, or prana, is another common definition, and as we alter our breathing patterns, we change our mental states in tangible ways.

Pratyahara, the first half of the word, *pratya*, means to "withdraw," "draw in," or "drawback," while the second part, *ahara*, denotes everything that we "take in" on our own, such as the many sights, sounds, and odors that our senses take in constantly. We tend to concentrate on 'drawing in' as our initial meditative act when we sit down for a structured meditation practice. This limb would also link directly to pranayama, the practice of regulating the breath, as part of the process of turning inward.

Dharana is a state of intense concentration. *Dha* means "holding" or "maintaining," while *Ana* means "other" or "something else." Dharana and pratyahara are integral elements of the same aspect and are inextricably tied to the preceding two limbs.

Dhyana is the seventh limb, or "meditative absorption," and it refers to the state of being fully immersed in the object of our meditation.

Samadhi, which many of us know to mean either "bliss" or "enlightenment," is the last destination of Patanjali's Yoga Sutras. The pinnacle of joy arrives when we have rearranged our connections with others and with ourselves.

According to the Katha Upanishad (written about 600 B.C.E.), the physical body is the chariot, the mind, and senses are the horses, and the soul is the charioteer. To do yoga is to master one's own thoughts and mental processes (Yogah Chitti Vritti Nirodah). *Tantra*, a branch of yoga, emerged about the year 1000 CE. These are said to awaken the "*Kundalini*," or snake energy, at the base of one's spine. *Hatha* yoga, a kind of yoga that emphasizes rigorous psychophysical practices to channel this energy, originated sometime between the first millennium CE and the second century CE. Since then, other hybrids of Raja and Hatha yoga have arisen, each with its unique emphasis on meditation, breath work, and physical postures.

Yoga is essential to a balanced and healthy lifestyle. All yoga asanas have a similar goal: improving one's health and well-being in body and mind. Yoga is a practice that can be done anywhere, at any time, and has several health advantages. One of yoga's greatest selling points is how easy it is to get started: all you need is a mat and 30 minutes a day. Different styles of yoga have entered the mainstream in recent years. Physical and mental health issues may both be helped by doing yoga. Therefore, it is incorrect to think that yoga is only practiced by members of a certain faith or ethnic group.

Yoga may be broken down into six distinct practices:

1. Hatha yoga
2. Ashtanga yoga

3. Vinyasa yoga
4. Kundalini yoga
5. Iyengar yoga

Hatha Yoga: The term "Hatha Yoga" comes from the Sanskrit word "*Hatha*," which means "force." Therefore, hatha yoga is effective in reestablishing internal equilibrium. The focus of this practice of yoga is on balancing the body's energy centers, or chakras. The seven chakras are located throughout the body and are linked to various glands and organs. Hatha yoga is the physical practice of balancing the body and the mind via a variety of postures and stances.

Ashtanga Yoga: An immediate descendant of Patanjali's Yoga Sutras is Ashtanga yoga. Ashtanga is a Sanskrit term derived from the word "eight," which explains the popularity of this yoga style for weight reduction. Principles, self-discipline, asana and postures, pranayama, withdrawal, focus, meditation, and salvation are the eight pillars of Ashtanga yoga.

Vinyasa Yoga: Commonly known as "flow" yoga, is a popular style of yoga. *Vi* means "variation" and *Nyasa* means "within prescribed limits," hence the term "Vinyasa" consists of these two concepts. Vinyasa is a style of yoga that combines physical motion with controlled breathing. The coordinated breathing and sequence of poses mimic the natural rhythm of living. For instance, Vinyasa yoga practitioners often start with a child's posture and end with savasana (the corpse position). If you want vigorous workouts, Vinyasa yoga is a fantastic option for you. Vinyasa yoga has several health benefits, including relief from stress, depression, high blood pressure, and insomnia.

Kundalini Yoga: This "yoga of awareness," is characterized by a series of postures that are repeated again and over. The dormant *Kundalini Shakti* is awakened by doing Kundalini yoga. The sacrum is the seat of one's spiritual force. *Kundalini Shakti*, according to yogis, lies dormant at the base of the spine like a coiled serpent. Therefore, vital energy rises with the spine and aids in your ethereal development. Stress, anxiety, sadness, and enhanced mental acuity are all treatable with Kundalini yoga.

Pranayama: *Pranayama* or deep, regulated breathing, comes after a chant to set the tone for the rest of the practice. Next is *kriya*, which consists of various yoga postures and mudras (a kind of hand gesture). The next step is to do meditation, chanting, and pranayama.

Iyengar Yoga: Another kind of yoga that's very close to *Vinyasa*. It was named after B.K.S. Iyengar, a world-renowned yoga master. When compared to other yoga traditions, Iyengar yoga stands out. Posture, alignment, and body-wide expansion are its primary foci. Additionally, yoga blocks and belts are used to help achieve the ideal positions. Musculoskeletal problems may be efficiently treated with Iyengar yoga, according to research. In addition, it has shown efficacy in the treatment of spinal impairments.

Sun Salutation/ Suryanamaskar

The sun salutation, also known as *Surya Namaskar*, is a popular yogic kriya. Even though it's a simple technique, its importance in the yoga community is enormous. In addition, you may do a high-intensity exercise in a fraction of the time it would take to perform 288 yoga postures. *Surya Namaskar* is most beneficial when performed at sunrise (between the hours of 4 and 7 a.m.).

Morning *Surya Namaskar* is a great way to wake up your body and mind. When performed at sunrise, *Surya namaskar* yields the greatest health advantages. Doing this first thing in the morning is a great way to wake up your brain and body. Your body will get the burst of stamina it needs to take on the day.

The Sun Salutation is a set of twelve distinct dynamic yoga postures that are performed in succession. If you've never done this before, start with three rounds, and then add one more every day. Prior to even beginning the exercises, I have provided you with some advice in the form of three recommendations to aid you.

- **Breathe:** Inhale and exhale with each yoga posture and activity, not only Surya Namaskar. Keep your breathing even and slow while you meditate.
- **Be consistent:** Maintain a routine of Surya Namaskar. This implies that to see effects in the long term, you need to adhere to it daily. Don't just throw it out after a few days.
- **Properly align:** A standard Surya namaskar for beginners consists of 12 positions. Pay close attention to how well each stance is aligned. Any deviation from perfect alignment increases the risk of injury and diminishes any potential advantages.

The Surya Namaskar may be performed in a variety of ways. The classic Hatha Surya Namaskara, though, is something I'd want to teach you.

The 12 movements (or asanas) that makeup *Surya Namaskar* are as follows:

1. *Pranamasana*, the Prayer Pose

Place your feet together at the top of your mat. Keep your back straight and your chest out. Pranayama (Namasté) is a yoga position in which you clasp your hands in the center of your chest after taking a deep breath in.

Benefits: The practice has several positive effects, including improved posture, the opening of the heart chakra, increased flexibility, aided digestion, and a calming effect on the mind and spirit.

2. *Hasta Uttanasana*, the Raised Arms Pose

Exhale as you bring your arms over your head and arch your back slightly towards the center.

Benefit: This asana is beneficial for those who suffer from back pain, exhaustion, and stress. People with asthma and gastrointestinal issues might benefit from it as well.

3. *Padahastasana*, the Standing Forward Bend Pose

Bend forward at the waist as you exhale and place your hands at your feet. Maintain a straight posture with your knees bent slightly.

Benefits: If you suffer from osteoporosis, you should try this asana. It's great for building leg and knee muscles. Improves flexibility in the thighs, hips, and legs. Those who suffer from headaches, anxiety, or stress can benefit from this asana.

4. Ashwa Sanchalanasana, the Lunge Pose

On your next inhale, get into a horse-riding position by bringing your right leg behind you.

Benefits: The result is increased lung capacity and spinal strength. The digestive tract, liver, and kidneys all benefit from it as well.

5. *Parvatasana*, the Mountain Pose

Bring your left leg behind you as you exhale. Keep your feet together for the time being. Stretch your legs out as far as you can and attempt to touch your heels to the mat

Benefits: It strengthens the spine and corrects spinal abnormalities. It also stretches and tones legs and arms.

6. Ashtanga Namaskar

Hold your breath and go on all fours, touching your knees, chest, and chin to the floor. The mat should be in contact with 8 points of your body, including your chin, chest, palms, knees, and feet.

Benefits: Improves bicep and tricep strength and overall arm and shoulder power. Benefits the back and spine by increasing their flexibility, stability, and range of motion.

7. Bhujangasana

Raise your body into a cobra posture as you inhale.

Benefits: Releases tension in the neck and upper back. Helps build strength in the upper body. Increases upper and mid-back mobility.

8. Parvatasana

Return to mountain posture on your next exhale.

Benefits: It aids the spinal cord and muscles by increasing flexibility and providing sufficient strength to go through the day without a hitch. The result is an increase in cerebral blood flow. The heart and lungs get a natural massage.

9. Ashwa Sanchalanasana, the Lunge Pose

As you inhale, come into a horse riding posture by bringing your right leg to the mat's top.

10. *Padahastasana*, the Standing Forward Bend Pose

Release your breath as you bring your left leg up to meet your right.

11. *Hasta Utthanasana*, the Raised Arms Pose

Raise your arms and take a deep breath in, while bending back.

12. *Pranamasana*, the Prayer Pose

Take a deep breath out and close your palms to namaste.

Repeat this process, this time beginning with your left leg. That concludes the first round.

Regular practice of Surya Namaskara burns fat, speeds up the circulatory rate, and tones all of the muscles and organs in the body. Six to 36 Surya Namaskars should be performed each morning.

Benefits of Yoga

Depression, anxiety, obsessive-compulsive disorder, and even schizophrenia have all demonstrated symptomatic improvements with regular yoga practice. The yoga-inspired relaxation activities and aerobic activities were also a part of the exercise intervention. A study reported that both the yoga and exercise groups had considerable improvements in their psychotic symptoms, however, the yoga group performed the best. Yoga has been demonstrated to be useful in reducing symptoms related to natural life stages in women, such as pregnancy and menopause, and studies have compared its effectiveness to exercise in unwell populations. Pregnant women who do yoga report more ease during their labor, while those going through menopause report fewer hot flashes. Both regular exercise and yoga have been shown to have positive psychological and physiological effects on study participants, although yoga is more effective in reducing physical symptoms and self-reported levels of stress.

I have shared a story below to help you understand the importance of yoga and flexibility.

> Once upon a time, India was a land of sages and rishis and people practiced yoga as a way of life. It was practiced on a day-to-day basis as a ritual. I have seen my father's flexibility in his joints and muscles as he used to sit in a cross-legged position to perform puja for long hours without any trouble. People spend a lot of money on gyms and are unaware of the benefits of simple yoga and stretching that can be done in the

comfort of their homes. Without any flexibility, there are chances of the muscles getting injured.

Hence, I would like to share a true incident that happened in my home. Whenever our loved ones and our people advise us we often take it for granted and ignore it. My son, Anish came from the United States to visit me in Dubai. He was studying engineering there and always aspired to be a great sportsman. He plays all the games like contact sports, football, and squash. He is a marathon runner and even plays golf. He goes to the gym regularly and maintains his six abs. His body physique is great. I was so proud of him for his routine workout. As usual, whenever he visited us during vacation, we used to keep a Satyanarayan Puja at home. We always advised Anish to do puja by sitting down on the ground. A young boy who was performing the puja the same age as Anish sat quickly on the ground with his legs crossed. When Anish tried to sit on the floor for puja, he could not come down easily on the floor, and bending his knees was very difficult for him. We were all surprised as such a fit boy could not sit on the floor comfortably as the Pandithji can!!

Then, I realized that his joints are stiff and his muscles are not stretched regularly. However, he completed the puja by sitting on a low stool chair.

After that, I asked him to practice yoga regularly for months and then the next time he visited us he could easily sit down on the floor to perform puja. Since then, he regularly practices yoga and he is very flexible now and muscle injuries are much less than before while playing sports.

Now, you might think that yoga is meant only for the young. Can the elderly also do yoga asanas?

Yoga rejuvenates your soul. Strengthens your entire body. Balances hormones and organs. Yoga is extremely important for all ages. Yoga asanas are one of the few workouts you may undertake as you age. As you become older, concentrate on how you do rather than how much.

Read on for some answers to frequently asked questions that I came across about how yoga might support healthy aging.

Table 7.1: Asanas for the elderly

Can someone above the age of 60 do yoga poses?	The Sanskrit root 'Yuj' means "to unite," which is whence the English term "yoga" was derived. **'Yoga is a study of life,'** explains Sri Sri Ravi Shankar. 'You study your body, your breath, your mind, your intellect, your memory, and your ego. Focus on developing your intuitive skills. Everyone, regardless of age or background, could gain something from doing yoga.
Which asanas are best for the elderly?	Yoga asanas may be performed in a variety of positions, including standing, sitting, laying down, and even on a chair.

What yoga poses are good for older individuals as beginners?	Sukshma yoga may be done alone or with other yoga styles. Seven minutes of sukshma yoga benefits everyone. It contains easy eye, jaw, neck, and hand movements.
How should the elderly do yoga?	The Patanjali Yoga Sutras call asana as "Sthira Sukham Asana." Asanas are stable and comfortable. Asanas are mindful, steady, and pleasant postures. Remember this while doing asanas.
How well do I seem to be doing at yoga?	The best person to decide this is you. Your internal gauge, the grin-o-meter, deserves a look. Do what you can and have a positive attitude about it. That is the gold standard for measuring success.
What are some of yoga's many advantages for the elderly?	<ul><li>Yoga is beneficial for maintaining joint stability and mobility.</li><li>Aids in the preservation of strong bones and muscles.</li><li>Facilitates bowel regularity and digestion.</li><li>Controls blood pressure levels.</li></ul>

What safety measures are recommended for elderly people?	• Walk and move instead of warming up. • Discuss your symptoms with a yoga instructor. • Repeat positions instead of holding them. • Recover between poses. • Before attempting new asanas, let your body acclimatize to yoga.

Here are some of the asanas for the elderly:

Standing Yoga Asanas

1. Trikonasana (Triangle Pose)
2. Katichakrasana (Standing spinal twist)

Sitting Yoga Asanas

1. Badhakonasana (Butterfly Pose)
2. Shishuasana (Child Pose)
3. Marjariasana (Cat-stretch Pose)

Yoga Poses Lying on the Back or Stomach

1. Bhujangasana (Cobra pose)
2. Shalabhasana (Locust posture)
3. Pawanmuktasana (Wind relieving pose)

Chair Yoga for Senior Citizens

Sitting asanas are handy for seniors and office workers. Neck roll, cow stretch, sitting forward bend, eagle arms, seated spinal twist, and temple massage are all beneficial chair yoga asanas.

Yoga Nidra or Yogic Sleep

Yoga Nidra is the most important element of yoga. As you age, assimilating its advantages becomes increasingly important.

Yoga, pranayama, and meditation can improve your life. Yoga improves your body and mind. Attitude will improve. You'll be young-minded. Remember, you're young!

With this, I want to share another real incident!

> Radha, my friend, a great economist went to a conference in Europe. The conference was great and her presentation was selected as the best. On the last day of the conference, the closing ceremony was held in the afternoon. It was a leisurely afternoon and the delegates were randomly asked to talk or present their own country's culture or anything that is best about their country. There were delegates from 20 nationalities and everyone was given 10 mins of time to present. Many of them spoke about the music, the landscapes, and the cuisines of their country. When Radha's turn came, she said rather than speaking I need to show you something. She gave a small introduction about India and yoga and then showed them the chair yoga pose. She showed how one can perform different yoga poses by just using a chair. Surprisingly, everybody at the conference performed chair yoga along with her. They all felt

> so great with those exercises and felt comfortable doing them. She also taught them breathing exercises along with it and they were all delighted. She became the hero of the conference and got special appreciation from the members of the conference.
>
> That is the essence of yoga.
>
> **'Simple but powerful'.**

However, there are a few guidelines to follow before, during, and after yoga asanas:

Before the Practice

- Yoga requires hygiene. It covers personal, environmental, and mental hygiene.
- Yoga should be done in a peaceful, relaxed state.
- Yoga should be practiced on an empty stomach.
- If you're weak, drink some honey with warm water.
- Yogic practices need an empty bladder and bowels.
- Practice on a mattress, yoga mat, or a folded blanket.
- To move freely, cotton garments are best.
- Yoga should not be done while exhausted, sick, rushed, or stressed.
- Before doing yoga, visit a doctor or yoga therapist if you have a chronic illness, discomfort, or cardiac issues.
- Pregnant and menstruating women should contact yoga specialists before practicing.

During the Practice

- Praying or invoking a higher power before practice helps set the tone and calms the mind.
- Yogic exercises are meant to be done at a leisurely pace, with full attention on the body and the breath.
- Breathe normally, and release your breath only when instructed to do so.
- Unless otherwise directed, breathe in and out via your nostrils only.
- At no stage should the body be held too firmly or jerked.
- Depending on your skill level, proceed with the exercises.
- Meditation/deep silence/ shanti patha is recommended as a closing practice for a yoga session.

After Practice

- After 20-30 minutes of training, you may take a bath.
- Only after you've trained for at least 20-30 minutes should you eat.

Take-Home Messages

> - Yoga is an ancient practice that aims to improve one's health on all levels: physical, mental, emotional, and spiritual.
> - Yoga is essential to a balanced and healthy lifestyle.
> - Asanas in yoga are among the few forms of exercise that may be maintained into old age.

- The many asanas practiced in yoga all work towards the same end: improving mental and bodily well-being.
- Physical and mental health issues may both be helped by doing yoga.
- One of the most popular and effective dynamic yoga poses is the Sun Salutation.
- Depression, anxiety, OCD, and even schizophrenia have all demonstrated symptomatic improvements with regular yoga practice.
- Pregnant women who do yoga report more ease during their labor, while those going through menopause report fewer hot flashes.

CHAPTER 8

The Best Style Is Ergonomics

Getting the ergonomics right.

Ergonomics refers to the science and practice of making tools, equipment, and environments more user-friendly. It's the study of how individuals function in an organizational setting. Ergonomics is the study of how to improve workplace conditions so that workers are less likely to sustain work-related ailments such as muscle strain, back pain, and postural deformities. Ergonomics is the study and application of how people use their bodies in the workplace to improve the safety and well-being of those people. The primary goal of ergonomics is the prevention or amelioration of work-related diseases and injuries.

Ergonomics, the study of how people interact with their work environments, is not only for office workers. The elderly may benefit from this for their overall health and happiness. Avoiding chronic pain later in life is one goal of ergonomics designed for the elderly. The next stage, if the elderly suffer from aches and pains, is applying ergonomics to facilitate normal activities such as opening a jam bottle, holding a jar, sitting, reading emails, and getting ready to go for a stroll. Reducing discomfort and making life simpler for the elderly is the goal of ergonomics, contemporary workplace furniture, and equipment.

Workplace conditions that contribute to unnecessary physical stress and potential harm are known as ergonomic risk factors. Some examples include prolonged sitting, standing in an uncomfortable position, moving too quickly, moving too slowly, and being subjected to direct pressure, vibration, temperature, noise, and stress at work. Force, repetition, and body position are three of the most important. Use of neutral posture, job rotation to prevent overuse injuries, adequate handholds and gripping technique, and proper lifting, carrying, pushing, and pulling processes are all examples of prominent ergonomic concepts.

There are three primary principles of ergonomics, and they are the following:

1. **Neutral postures:** A neutral posture allows the spine to keep its natural curvature while yet being in a healthy position.
2. **Reduce excessive force:** Lessen the amount of force you use to push, pull, or move big objects since doing so might cause weariness and even damage. Find ways to reduce the weight you have to carry and do it without resorting to unnecessary force.
3. **Keep things easy to reach:** Try making a half circle with your arms outstretched in front of you. Your reach envelope is the half-circle at your desk where you should keep the things you use most often.

OSHA GUIDELINES: Computer workstations

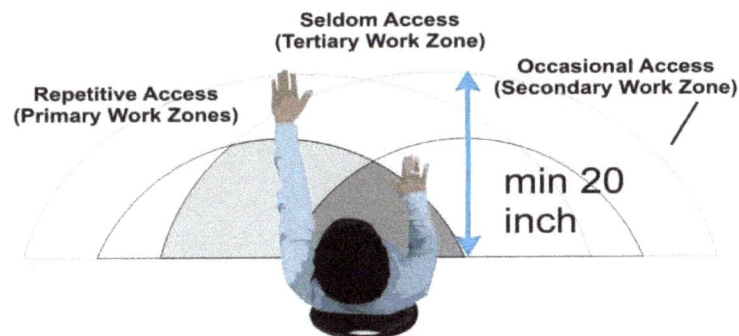

Fig 8.1 Recommended zones for the workplace

Some of the **key elements** of ergonomics are listed below:

1. Identifying hazard
2. Decreasing the potential for harm
3. Risk mitigation verification
4. Controlling mishaps
5. Ensure the long-term viability of the program
6. Putting the ergonomics plan into action

Ergonomics is a technique used to improve safety and productivity in physically demanding tasks. Findings indicate that true staff engagement and long-term dedication are necessary for a successful implementation of ergonomics.

It is still true that the elderly need extra attention from attentive care givers. Ergonomics focuses primarily on ensuring the highest level of safety for the elderly when they move about the environment, sit, stand, and use the lavatory. Some guidelines for protecting the elderly are provided below.

1. Seating

Many older people have problems bending their knees because of arthritis or brittle bones while they are trying to find a comfortable place to sit. It becomes uncomfortable to sit on a typical chair or couch. Chairs with height adjustment are essential for the elderly in terms of ergonomic design. When sitting to type or write, this might be as comfortable as a regular office chair. A high back is essential for the support of an older person in an ergonomic chair. High-back chairs assist the elderly navigate about the room without the need for a cane or walker.

To prevent the elderly from sinking into the couches, the seating must be soft yet supportive. It may be difficult to rise from such couches. When reading a book or newspaper, armrests are a welcome addition for the elderly.

2. Walking / Movement

Keep any passageways clear of anything that may slow people down. It is important to have clear pathways from flooring that is both supporting and not too smooth, making it easier to walk or use a wheelchair. Make sure all of the hallways and doorways are well-lit. The signs and room numbers are illuminated so that they may be read easily. Such signs are required to be hung at a level readable by the average human. The elderly would benefit greatly from railings or grab bars installed on each side of the hallway. It's ideal if the floor is nonslippery. Staircases should be avoided if at all feasible.

The same rule applies to restrooms and utilizing them. There is a significant and urgent need for a handrail. As long as there is a grab bar nearby, many seniors will stubbornly refuse assistance while getting off the toilet.

3. Standing

Standing desks are highly suggested for all computer users. Why? Each user may adjust the height of their standing desk to work while standing up. They may stand while working, or lower it to sit. A standing desk might be provided for those who want to avoid sitting while reading newspapers or working with a computer. If you prefer to use a wheelchair or regular office chair while you work, you may adjust the height of a standing desk to meet your needs.

4. Holding

It's important to keep the elderly in mind while designing ergonomic gear. The handle should be comfortable to hold. Hot pans need cool grips. As a result, less heat will be transferred to your food during consumption. Elderly people benefit from lighter, more compact tools and tableware.

5. Safety

All furniture and decorative items must have smooth, rounded edges to prevent injury, even inadvertent ones. The use of cushiony materials that can absorb impact is important. Slick flooring should be avoided if at all possible. Those who use wheelchairs or roller walking sticks, however, will benefit more from a surface with a greater coefficient of friction. Nursing facilities benefit the most from resilient flooring options including rubber, linoleum, and tile. Why? This is because most people have a better experience holding onto these materials.

Most controls, including handles and levers, should be positioned at waist height, making them easily accessible to the elderly, whether they are seated in a wheelchair or not.

6. Lighting

Poor illumination is a major contributor to senior accident rates. What most of us would consider to be adequate lighting can be too dim for the elderly. Why? Age often results in diminished eyesight. Ambient illumination should be improved, particularly in places where movement is difficult, as part of senior ergonomics to help prevent falls and improve visibility.

The aged population has a greater ergonomics requirement than the general population. Their well-being and safety are paramount as they go about their daily routines. The importance of ergonomics does not decline with age. Ergonomics is here to make everything you do easier and more pleasant.

Here are eight impressive benefits of ergonomics in the workplace.

1. Health Benefits

Ergonomic workplaces are better for the health of the people who work there. The effects of ergonomics may be felt first in the heart, and then travel throughout the body. In comparison to working in a more typical setting, your heart health will improve. Maintaining a neutral posture may relieve tension in the eyes, neck, and back. Increased circulation will also aid your legs.

2. Improved Productivity

Efficacy and comfort go hand in hand in an ergonomic workplace. Ergonomic workstations make use of several organizational and technological innovations to boost productivity in the workplace. When workers' workspace is well-designed, they are less likely to get sidetracked by issues like pain or disorganization.

3. Improved Mental Clarity

You'll be able to think more clearly and get more done if you eliminate distractions and straighten up your body. As a bonus, ergonomics might help you relax and focus better at work. When you're relaxed, you're better able to concentrate. Ergonomics is useful since it lessens discomfort, builds up muscle, and boosts circulation. As a whole, this may help you think more clearly.

4. Decreased Pains

Having ergonomically built seats, desks, and other furniture and adjustable workstations may also aid improve posture and lessen the risk of musculoskeletal ailments like back discomfort. Employers may do their part to keep workers healthy and in peak working conditions by providing an ergonomically sound workplace.

5. Eliminating Hazards

Reducing the risks that workers face daily is an important part of making the workplace safer and more productive. Ergonomics is the study of how people work, intending to design safer and more efficient workplaces. Workplace risks may be reduced or eliminated because of the contributions of ergonomics in areas like noise reduction, lighting, ventilation, and the design of ergonomic furniture and tools.

8. Focus on Safety

Ergonomics will raise awareness and make the workplace safer. You will eliminate dangers, make workplaces more comfortable, and instruct your co-workers on how to make their own environments safer.

Early Warning Signs of Poor Ergonomics Among Computer Users

Poor ergonomic practices when using a computer may inflict strain on muscles, tendons, and nerves by making the same motions over and over again which can ultimately lead to Repetitive stress injury (RSI). Repetitive stress injuries (RSIs) are described as deficits in muscles, tendons, and nerves that are produced, induced, or worsened by repetitive movement of the body during work. It is widespread among those who use computers. Repetitive stress injury also known as computer-related injury (CRI), occurs in 3 different phases:

Stage 1: Work-related pain that subsides when you stop working; full recovery in a matter of weeks.

Stage 2: Acute pain that lasts during the day but subsides overnight; a lengthy recovery time (months)

Stage 3: Pain that keeps you awake at night and lingers during the day; a lengthy recovery time (months to a year)

Below are some of the different forms of RSI:

- Myofascial Pain Syndrome (MPS)
- Thoracic Outlet Syndrome (TOS)
- Carpal tunnel Syndrome (CTS)
- Cubital Tunnel Syndrome (CTS)

Prevalence: Researchers in India analyzed almost a thousand computer experts to determine the incidence of repetitive stress injury (RSI) and associated risk variables. Myofascial pain syndrome was found to affect 80% of responders, Thoracic outlet syndrome affected 50%, fibromyalgia affected 30%, wrist tendinitis affected 8%, complex regional pain syndrome affected 5%, and cubital tunnel syndrome affected 5%.

Nevertheless, being aware of the precursors of a crisis is essential for effective management. Here are a few potential red flags:

- Problems with clenching and unclenching your fists
- Weakness and Exhaustion
- Trembling and Stiffness
- Avoiding handshakes
- Problems manipulating objects (like a book)
- Regular self-massage
- Slumping about, especially as the day ends down
- Awakening in discomfort or numbness
- Medications in bottles on the workstation
- Variations in output or quality that are out of the ordinary

However, there are some risk factors of RSI that cannot be ignored. They are the following:

- RSI was strongly linked to poor ergonomics 53.50 percent of the time.

- Stress was linked to RSI 38% of the time.
- Lack of breaks was associated with it 63% of the time.

Diagnosis of RSI

You should speak to your doctor about RSI if you're experiencing any pain or difficulty doing routine chores at work or at home. Your doctor will inquire as to your employment and leisure hobbies in an effort to determine whether you engage in any repetitive motions. They will also inquire as to the nature of your workstation and whether or not you use a computer there. They will also do a physical examination. The examination will include assessments of a range of motion in addition to evaluations of localized discomfort, inflammation, reflexes, and strength.

If your doctor suspects tissue injury, he or she may recommend an MRI or ultrasound. A doctor may recommend an electromyography (EMG) to assess muscle and nerve function. Your doctor may suggest seeing a physical therapist if your injuries are very minor. A specialist or surgeon may be recommended if the damage is extensive.

Treatments for RSI

A professional physiotherapist is the only one who can help you. I've included several phased approaches to treating RSI below.

Phase I

Severe discomfort: Soft tissue manipulation indirect techniques, myofascial release, relaxation techniques, breathing exercise

Phase II

Moderate discomfort: Soft tissue, neuro-dynamic & articular mobilization, self-stretching exercises, Alexander technique, and Yoga

Phase III

Mild discomfort: Stretching exercises, progressive strengthening, postural retraining, body mechanics, and ergonomics training

Phase IV

Maintenance: Further strength training, aerobic conditioning, and Yoga

Phase V

Prevention of re-occurrence

In addition, the health advantages that come with ergonomics help to keep workers healthy while they are on the job. As a bonus, this will promote security. Precautions based on principles of ergonomics may make homes for the elderly safer and more pleasant places to spend time. Here are some age-related issues and some ergonomic approaches to addressing them.

1. Spine Issues

One needs to use a chair with a backrest that provides proper lumbar support. It's important to have a computer or television screen at eye level while using it. Always maintain a healthy posture by sitting up straight or by adjusting the chair's arm and back supports.

3. Muscle Strain

Taking ergonomic measures may help reduce the risk of muscular strain. A torn muscle is often the consequence of rapid movement, which may be avoided by using an ergonomically designed workplace, kitchen table, restroom, sitting arrangement, and furnishings.

4. Knee Pain

The knee is the largest and heaviest-bearing joint in the human body. Consequently, maintenance is crucial. If you're going to be sitting for lengthy periods, whether in your bedroom, home office, or TV room, invest in an ergonomic chair. You need to be able to lean back comfortably in the chair and get your legs flat on the floor or the footrest.

5. Neck pain

Avoiding neck discomfort when using a computer or watching television requires the appropriate posture. When working on a computer, it's best to do so from a height-adjustable chair. You should be looking down at the screen from approximately arm's length away. Use a recliner with appropriate lumbar support and a comfortable viewing angle while watching television or a movie in the comfort of your own home.

6. Sore Shoulders

Shoulder discomfort may be alleviated and future episodes avoided with the aid of ergonomics. Keep the 90-degree rule in mind when you arrange your loved one's home office. Seating that supports your back and neck is recommended.

7. Ache in the Wrist

If your loved one spends a lot of time at a computer, you should get them some wrist pads. To avoid straining or spraining their wrist muscles, keep frequently used objects like light switches, silverware, and clothing within easy reach. Use light seats and stools to prevent wrist injuries. Avoiding wrist injuries is another benefit of using silverware designed for people with arthritis.

Ergonomics, as you can see, is applicable outside of the workplace as well. The elderly, whether they live independently or are cared for, may also gain much from the use of ergonomic methods and equipment. Every room in the house, from the kitchen to the home theatre, may benefit from ergonomic design.

Benefits of Ergonomics for Elders

Ease of use: Many elderly people struggle with using kitchenware, appliances, and instruments due to illnesses such as arthritis. However, ergonomics provides convenience for those with these issues.

Comfort: Ease of use, in turn, helps improve the comfort of the elderly by reducing the distress brought on by preexisting medical issues. With improved ease of living, your loved ones may continue to thrive and participate in life on their own.

Safety: Ergonomics makes your home a safer place for your family to live. It may lessen the likelihood of slip-and-fall incidents.

Now that you are aware of the benefits of Ergonomics, I would like to share a simple story to remind you all that even a little change at a workstation or place can change your life.

As a rehabilitation consultant, I look after people well-being and work on the principle of **"early care is the better cure."** In that context, I often do Ergonomics consultations in Multinational companies and do take multiple lectures on Ergonomics. I help people to set their offices Ergonomically friendly so that people working in the office for long hours of time have a quality working area. People suffer from neck and back pain sitting for long hours on stiff chairs. You can avoid all these pains by simply adopting ergonomic principles.

I remember that it was a Monday morning, 5 years ago. I was called to one of the famous multinational companies for an Ergonomics lecture. I finished my lecture and as usual, people were happy with the presentation and solutions that I provided. Suddenly I saw a tall guy who happened to be the general manager of the company, standing at the door and sarcastically laughing at me. I went to him and asked, "Mr. Jacob, why are you laughing at me, did you not find this presentation useful to you?". He was from Europe and he said, 6 months back he had disc compression surgery for disc prolapse in the lower lumbar region. He said that after the surgery also he gets severe back pain if he sits for long hours in the chair. I asked him to show me his chair. When I assessed the chair, I found out that it was an ergonomically poor chair. The chair height was low, the seat was hard and uncomfortable which was giving an upward push on the spine which led to the increase in pain. He told me that he cannot change his costly chair. But then, I suggested to him a very simple solution which is using an exercise ball. I told him to use an exercise ball of 85 cm and to sit on it for some time during the day, which can gradually decrease the pressure on his back. I then left the office and forgot about this incident.

After six months I was again called for a lecture in the same office to address the new joiners. As I was entering the office the old employees greeted me and looked at me differently. I was wondering what was happening and then someone told me that Mr. Jacob is waiting for me in the conference room. I went there to see him and I was surprised to see 20 exercise balls lying in the room. Mr. Jacob greeted me and told me that sitting on the ball for long hours during the meetings reduced his back pain and so he insisted all the managers sit on the balls during long meetings. He also changed his chair and replaced it with an ergonomic chair. He thanked me immensely for this simple change that eventually cured his back pain.

With this story, it is evident that a **Simple ergonomic solution can do wonders.**

The Dual Role of Ergonomics

Ergonomics, as I've already indicated, is relevant to individuals of all ages. It's not only for domestic use; it may be a crucial component in commercial settings as well. Many businesses have been allowing their employees to work from home in response to the current COVID-19 epidemic. However, it has had a drastic change in the health of many. Employees' health might suffer if they were required to work from home without a proper office setup. Working from home has been linked to an increased risk of low back pain (LBP) in several studies. The goal of ergonomics is to maximize efficiency and comfort in the workplace. That work might be something done in the office or at home. Here are some tips to assist you straighten up your back and make your everyday routines more comfortable.

1. **Practice proper workplace ergonomics:** Maintain correct posture when sitting on a chair for long periods. Keep your back straight and your chin high. Ensure that your hips and shoulders are in a straight line.
2. **Posture:** Improve your daily posture and ergonomics by raising your awareness of these factors. When lifting, sitting, doing repeated activities, or working in uncomfortable bodily postures, remember to be attentive.
3. **The 20-20-20 rule:** Take a 20-second break every 20 minutes and look away from your screen at least 20 feet away

Ergonomic and lifestyle adjustments may help you operate more efficiently, feel less tired, and recover from muscular strain faster.

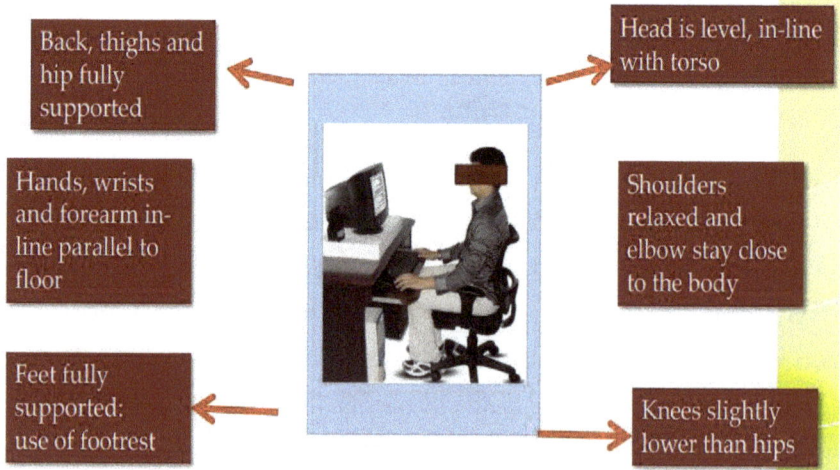

Fig 8.2 Good working posture

The human body is a living entity that functions best when used. However, many individuals now spend their days sitting at a desk in front of a computer. Common workplace stances aren't exactly healthy. Sedentary work and bad posture, when added to an inactive lifestyle, may have devastating long-term effects on both physical and mental health. When we adopt a stance for work that is not ergonomic, we subject our bodies to unnecessary stress. Physical consequences may include, but are not limited to, the following:

- Prolonged sitting puts a heavy burden on the body's joints. The lumbar area and the neck are the worst-hit regions
- Less adaptability
- Lowered blood flow
- Because extended sitting compresses the organs, digestion is impaired
- Potential for the onset of chronic pain, which may have negative impacts on mental health and quality of life
- Furthermore, a sedentary lifestyle (defined as fewer than 150 minutes of moderate physical exercise each week) is linked to an increased risk of acquiring several illnesses such as diabetes, certain types of cancers, etc.

Inadequate ergonomic practices among computer users are associated with the following:

- Misaligned monitor (60% of cases)
- Too high of a mouse (54%).
- Having a solid surface under the arm or wrist as it types (42%).
- The height of the keyboard is too much (40%).

- Absurd leg posture (25%)
- Considerations for lighting, glare, airflow, and climate
- Job scheduling, workload, and organization
- Factors such as age, sex, muscularity, pliability, anatomy, and muscle tension habits
- Use of a computer at home, lack of exercise, and a history of health problems that predispose to illness

I have included several overarching **risk factors** that everyone, from at-home retirees to working individuals, should keep an eye on:

- Discomforting postures
- Bending
- Forces of contact or compression
- Exertion of force
- Lack of enough pauses/breaks
- Lifting
- Noise
- Struggle, tension
- Habitual behaviors
- Static or prolonged positions
- Extremes in temperature
- Vibration

Even if the workstation is well-designed and the surrounding conditions are optimal, workers still need to be mindful of their bodies and use proper ergonomic practices while they're on the job. If you don't practice good ergonomics and keep an eye out for warning indications, little issues might escalate into major injuries!

Treatment for Ergonomic Injuries

Eventually, a cure will be found for every known illness. Similarly, there are therapies or treatments available for injuries that may be traced back to improper Ergonomics. On the job front, having access to on-site treatment alternatives may help. One advantage of on-site therapy is that the physical therapist may visit the workplace, learn the specifics of the patient's posture, and make appropriate ergonomic adjustments based on what they see. A physical therapist can help with injuries suffered by seniors due to poor ergonomics. As a first line of defense, people may try over-the-counter pain relievers and non-invasive therapies like cold packs and compression. If the discomfort continues, though, you might think about making a doctor's appointment.

In addition to these considerations, it might be helpful to practice good ergonomics and adhere to a strengthening and flexibility training routine. Keep an eye out for the warning signs and try to incorporate ergonomic concepts into your routine.

Prevention is better than cure!

Self-Assessment

- Do you follow proper ergonomics? (Be it at home or workspace)
- Are you aware of the signs and symptoms of computer-related injuries?

- Do you follow the 20-20-20 rule?
- Are you vigilant of the health-related consequence of poor ergonomics?
- Are you taking the necessary precautions to prevent ergonomic-related musculoskeletal problems?

Take-Home Messages

- Do not 'IGNORE' ergonomics.
- Ergonomics is a study of people at work, it includes both office and at home.
- Incorporating ergonomics and lifestyle changes into your workplace and life can increase productivity, decrease fatigue and decrease muscle soreness.
- Failing to apply ergonomic principles and recognize early warning signs could allow small problems to develop into serious injuries!
- **A simple ergonomic solution can do wonders.**
- Ergonomics is never limited to the age of an individual.

CHAPTER 9

Just Let Your Stress Fly Away

Embrace Movement: Your Key to Stress Relief

Stress is a condition of concern or mental strain brought on by a demanding circumstance. Stress is a normal human reaction that forces us to deal with adversity. Stress is a part of life for everyone. However, the degree to which we react positively or negatively to stress has a significant impact on our health. There are several ways in which stress may modify how we feel, how we act, and how our bodies function. When we're under pressure, it might be easy to notice it right away. On the other hand, there are occasions when we may choose to ignore the warnings and go on.

What are the symptoms of stress?

- Irritable, angry, and impatient
- Over-burdened or overwhelmed
- Anxious, nervous, or afraid
- Unable to enjoy yourself
- Depressed
- Uninterested in life
- A sense of dread

- Worried or tense
- Neglected or lonely
- Existing mental health problems getting worse

How does stress affect us?

The effects of stress extend beyond the mental realm. A healthy dose of stress may motivate us to get through the day. The effects of stress on the body and the mind are real. One's emotional and physical health may benefit from learning effective stress management techniques.

What are the treatments for stress?

There is no medically accepted way to diagnose stress and no one therapy that is guaranteed to work for everyone. Changing the source of stress, learning how to manage it, practicing relaxation methods, and treating any resulting symptoms or disorders are all part of the treatment process. Therapy, medication, and complementary and alternative medicine (CAM) are all options that deserve consideration.

How do I manage stress?

- **Keep a daily routine:** Keeping to a routine may help us make better use of our time and give us a sense of mastery over our lives. Schedule time for regular meals, family time, exercise, household tasks, and fun activities.
- **Get a good night's rest**: The body and mind benefit from quality sleep. Repairing, de-stressing, and rejuvenating

when sleeping may help counteract the harmful effects of stress.
- Maintaining a regular bedtime and rising time (even on the weekends) is very important.
- Make sure your bedroom is as peaceful, dark, and has a comfortable temperature as possible.
- Avoid using TVs, laptops, and smartphones an hour or so before bedtime if possible.
- Avoid coffee and alcohol if you want a good night's sleep.
- The ability to drift off to sleep at night improves with regular physical activity throughout the day.
- **Connect with others:** Stay in contact with loved ones and close friends, and talk about what's on your mind with those you can trust. Having meaningful interactions with others has been shown to improve mood and reduce stress.
- **Watch your diet:** What we put into our bodies has an impact on how we feel and perform. Maintain a regular eating schedule and eat healthily. Take in sufficient fluids. If you have the option, fill your diet with fresh produce.

Get Moving to Manage Stress

Any kind of physical activity may help reduce stress. Exercising releases endorphins, which make you feel good and take your mind off of your problems. Any kind of physical activity, from aerobics to yoga, may help you relax and unwind. You don't need to be an athlete or even very fit to benefit much from exercise for stress management. Learn how exercise may help you relax and de-stress, and why it should form part of your strategy for dealing with stress.

Exercising is a Great Way to Relieve Stress

In addition to improving your health and mood, regular exercise also gives you extra energy. However, there are certain clear ways in which physical activity might reduce stress.

Raised Serotonin and Dopamine Levels

The release of endorphins, the brain's "feel good" neurotransmitters, may be stimulated by engaging in physical exercise. This effect is often associated with running, although it may be achieved via any cardiovascular exercise, such as a spirited game of tennis or a peaceful stroll in the woods. The harmful consequences of stress are mitigated. Physical activity has been shown to reduce stress by simulating the physical impacts of stress—such as the body's "flight or fight" response—and so giving the body and its systems valuable experience operating together in stressful situations. This may help shield your body from the negative impacts of stress, which in turn benefits your cardiovascular, digestive, and immunological systems.

Below, I have listed some of the exercises that you can follow to reduce stress:

1. High-Energy Activities

The heart rate rises with vigorous physical activity including running, dancing, spinning, and in-line roller skating. Endorphins, the body's natural opiates, are released at a high enough heart rate to make you feel happy without any negative consequences.

2. Yoga

Yoga is a great way to relax since it combines controlled breathing with a sequence of physical postures (both dynamic and static).

The other top stress-relieving activities are listed below:

- Walking quickly
- Jogging or running
- Swimming, cycling, or dancing
- Boxing
- High-intensity interval training

High-functioning depression (HFD)

People who live with high-functioning depression, also known as dysthymia, are often high achievers who give the impression that everything is well all of the time. This may make high-functioning depression more difficult to diagnose than major depressive disorder (MDD), which is a more common form of depression. Extreme stress has also been linked to high-functioning depression (HFD). Depression that isn't severe enough to warrant a professional diagnosis is often referred to as "high-functioning." A person with functional depression may feel sad or unmotivated yet be able to go about their normal routine. Someone with this diagnosis is able to manage their symptoms of depression effectively enough to have positive relationships, careers, and personal lives. It is important to recognize that high-functioning depression is a legitimate condition that, if left unaddressed and untreated, may have major repercussions. Officially, high-functioning depression is referred to as persistent depressive disorder or PDD for short. PDD sufferers exhibit many of the symptoms of depression, but on a milder scale than those who struggle with depression. This enables the individual to be able to operate generally regularly, including going to work or school, doing well, keeping up with chores at home, and participating in the majority of social events. A moderate form of persistent depression disorder (PDD), which is diagnosable and curable, may be present in someone with excellent functioning but also signs of poor mood. Long-term depression symptoms are characteristic of PDD, also known as dysthymic disorder. In other instances, research has shown that the severity of a mental illness may be less severe, and a person may be able to continue to operate normally, or nearly normal, most of the time while still having symptoms associated with the condition. This is what people mean when they talk about a high-functioning individual having a mental illness. It is essential to keep in mind that high-functioning is not synonymous with fully functioning in this context. There is still some level of impairment while dealing with this kind of depression. The state of being able to operate normally but continuing to endure major depressive symptoms is what's referred to as persistent depressive illness (PDD). In the past, those who suffered from this mental disorder were diagnosed with dysthymia, and some people still use that word today

How do we manage HFD?

There is no such thing as a depression remedy that can be achieved via physical activity alone. However, a significant body of evidence suggests that regular exercise may help alleviate or even prevent symptoms of depression and help people suffering from high-functioning depression. Exercising seems to have significant positive effects on the mental health of those suffering from depression and other disorders of a similar kind such as HFD. Physical activity has been shown to raise levels of some chemicals in the brain, including those that promote the growth of new brain cells and new connections between existing brain cells.

In addition to the direct impacts that exercise has on the brain, additional physical changes that occur as a result of exercise, such as enhanced cardiovascular fitness and improved metabolic health, boost brain health in an indirect manner. Following are some of the exercises to manage HFD.

1. **Go for a Run for an all-natural mood boost:** The Endorphins released during a jog will reduce your perception of pain and trigger a positive feeling in the body.
2. **Lift mood by lifting some weights:** According to a research strength-training exercises also help relieve symptoms of depression.
3. **Combine Yoga with other treatments to feel even better:** Research has shown that practicing yoga is another activity that can ease symptoms of depression, especially when combined with usual treatment, such as cognitive behavioral therapy.
4. **Walk regularly to help ease the blues:** Walking is an aerobic exercise that is suited for almost everyone and thus helps manage depressive symptoms.

Some suggestions for managing high-functioning disorders are the following:

- Talk to a therapist
- **Add exercise to your routine:** Incorporate regular physical activity into your schedule, as recommended by your doctor. The benefits of exercise on people of all ages' mental and emotional well-being have been well-documented. This is especially true for those who suffer from PDD and other forms of chronic moderate depression, as well as those who suffer from depression brought on by persistent worry.
- **Create a daily plan of action:** To improve one's feeling of self-worth and motivation, it's helpful to establish frequent, manageable objectives.
- **Mind what you eat:** A change in diet should be accompanied by increased vitality, less fatigue, and sharpened mental clarity.
- **Set a regular schedule for bedtime and wake time:** Better sleep habits have been linked to better mental and physical health.
- **Reduce or abstain from using drugs and alcohol based on individual risk factors:** If you need help recovering from drug usage, you should get it.
- **Reach out to others:** Talk to close ones, individuals you know in real life and online, support groups, and other resources that may help you feel better.

The Joy of Movement

Alexander Bain, a Scottish philosopher, coined the term "runner's high" in 1885 to describe the sensation of happiness and euphoria that comes on after a lengthy period of running or jogging. Today, we call this sensation the "runner's high." This high has been linked to anything from falling in love to the effects of various types of mind-altering substances.

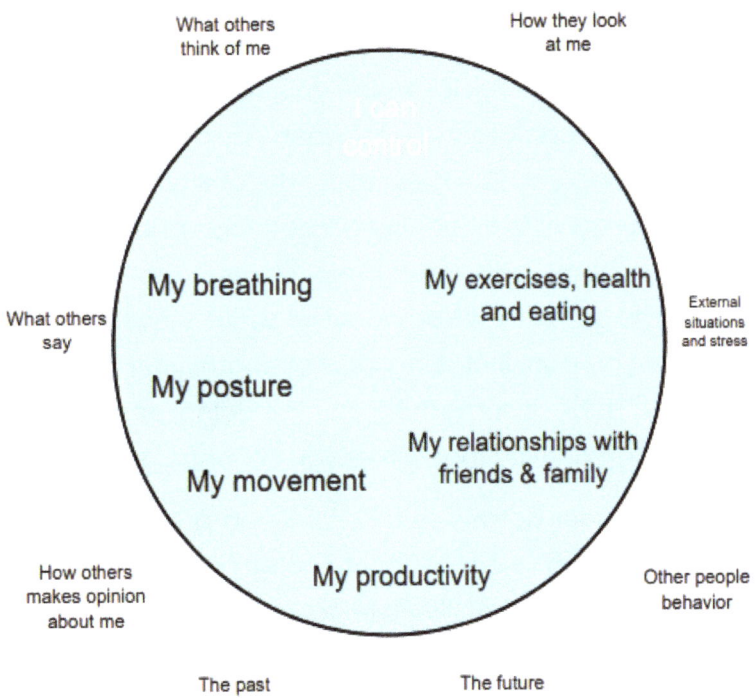

Fig 9.1 Illustration on the joy of movement and self-control

Recent research has shown that going for a long run significantly boosts the number of endocannabinoids that are present in our brains. The effects that these compounds have on the brain are mimicked by cannabis, which is a family of chemicals. Endocannabinoids are renowned for their ability to reduce pain, increase mood, and cause the release of other chemicals and neurotransmitters that provide a positive feeling, such as dopamine and endorphins. Additionally, Endocannabinoids assist in warding off anxiousness and sadness. Therefore, the burst of brain chemicals that occurs as a result of sustained physical activity may be more appropriately referred to as a "persistence high."

The satisfaction that comes from moving your body comes from loving how you feel when you go for a run, as well as how you feel after doing yoga or tai chi. It's where you put your body to use to interact with the world around you. When you connect with other individuals is when you feel most alive. The ability to move about is vital to the human condition. Joy will be known and experienced by both your body and your brain as you move. The only advantage you get comes from moving about. Utilize as much of your body as you can, including your strength, your vitality, and your flexibility. Think of something you like doing, and then try to come up with an activity that will let you continue doing it.

You should consider activity to be a vital component of your life, on par with the need to eat and get enough sleep. When you go from having a sedentary lifestyle to one that requires more activity, your brain goes through a number of changes. At the very least, six weeks of consistent exercise are required for your brain to start rewarding you for your efforts. You should constantly try to mix activity with something that you like doing and that also keeps your interest. You should first pay some attention to what you are feeling with your body when it is in movement, and you must embrace the bodily sensations of the feedback from different parts of your body such as the muscles, which tell you that they are feeling good. This will help you feel the joy that movement can bring, as well as relieve anxiety and depression.

The most effective treatment for relieving stress and anxiety is physical activity. Dopamine, endocannabinoid, and endorphin receptors are made more readily available in the brain as a result of physical activity. These receptors are responsible for the feelings of pleasure and optimism that are induced by exercise. There is no such thing as too little physical activity in order to reap the mental and physical advantages. Any slightest movement you do can bring you joy. However, those who are struggling with issues related to their mental health should keep in mind that they should not be scared to push themselves beyond the limits of what they believe they are capable of. Always make an effort to spend some time in the fresh air or greenery around you. It will assist you in achieving mental bliss, psychological equilibrium, and the advantages of movement.

Take-Home Messages

- Stress is a part of life, however, it can have a negative effect on your overall health if ignored.
- Do watch out for high-functioning depression (HFD) and persistent depressive disorder (PDD).
- The only good medicine is following an exercise regime and quality sleep.
- Always remember the phrase **"get moving to manage stress."**
- The ability to move about is essential to the functioning of the human body.
- Physical activity is the only treatment that may alleviate the symptoms of mental health problems.

CHAPTER 10

Healthy is New Happy

Happiness is the highest form of health.

How does happiness impact health?

Happiness is beneficial. It gives us confidence, a "take on the world" mentality, and an upbeat spirit that may reflect on others. Recent research suggests that there are three paths to fulfillment: helping others, developing your strengths, and prioritizing your own needs. Optimists, in particular, tend to be happy people.

Health Consequences

Being joyful has positive effects on our bodies and minds. We are able to eat better, exercise more, and get better rest as a result. Most individuals define happiness as having a good time and feeling well. There are several ways in which a person's mental and physical well-being might benefit by adopting a more optimistic outlook.

- A person's health and happiness depend on their ability to maintain an optimistic and active outlook.
- **Enhancing one's capacity to solve problems:** People with a positive outlook feel they "can" and are motivated to succeed.

- **Keeping yourself healthy:** The risks of cardiovascular illness, high blood pressure, poor sleep quality, poor nutrition, being overweight, and not exercising regularly are all reduced when people report higher levels of happiness.
- Being happy reduces the risk of stroke by preventing hypertension and obesity.
- Being happy makes your immune system stronger.
- The positive effects of happiness extend to warding off stress, illness, and impairment.
- When we're happy, we live longer.

Your health is not a mystery and neither should it be. Find out what makes you happy and what doesn't, then do more of what makes you happy. Accept your decisions and move forward. Your health relies on happiness.

Pleasure versus Happiness

To what extent do you equate happiness with experiencing pleasure? Despite their apparent similarities, they are distinct concepts.

What is pleasure?

Pleasure may be both mental and physical, and it often involves all five senses. It's temporary and attainable by physical means such as objects. Substance or objects and behavioral addiction both begin at the extremes of pleasure. Dopamine, the "pleasure biochemical" or "neurotransmitter," is ultimately responsible for feelings of satisfaction.

What is happiness?

Happiness comes in a variety of forms. It's not something you can experience with your five senses; it comes from within. A cheerful person is one who is in a state of happiness. This is a way of thinking rather than a response to anything happening in the outside world. Genuine contentment originates inside. A person who has found lasting joy in life may look back with gratitude and contentment. Objects are not a route to happiness. The neurotransmitter and molecule linked to happiness is called serotonin.

Happiness and Exercise

Your body and your mind both benefit immensely from regular exercise. Endorphins, dopamine, adrenaline, and endocannabinoids are all brain chemicals that are related to feeling joyful, feeling confident, feeling competent, feeling less anxious and stressed, and even experiencing less physical pain. When you exercise, these brain chemicals are increased, which causes you to experience all of these things. Getting regular exercise not only makes people happier and better off physically, but it also helps them feel less anxious and depressed.

According to research conducted at the University of Michigan, more physical activity is associated with increased levels of happiness; however, even brief bouts of exercise have been shown to have good effects. The fact that physical activity is an experience rather than a commodity to be acquired also contributes to happiness. Research conducted by the University of Texas found that individuals report much higher levels of happiness when they invested in experiences rather than material possessions. Participating in activities that promote physical fitness often results in experiences that are more challenging and demanding as well as more satisfying.

The Best Ways to Exercise

Here are some tips to help you maximize your workouts whenever and wherever you do your job

- **Do what you love (DWYL):** Popular forms of physical activity nowadays include weight training, yoga, cycling, Pilates, barre, boxing, gym sessions, jogging, streaming yoga, and dancing.
- Running, in particular, has been found to increase mood and cognitive function according to a study by the University of Tsukuba.
- When stressed you can choose boot camps, HIT classes, or indoor cycling.
- Pilates, yoga, and ballet are popular choices for those who want to unwind after a busy day.
- **Yoga:** Yoga has been shown to lessen feelings of despair and increase feelings of optimism, according to a study conducted at the Boston University Medical Centre.
- **Work out with others:** Positive emotions are strongly linked to the quality of one's social relationships. The greatest happiness comes from doing things with other people.
- **Aerobics:** A successful completion of a 45-min aerobic session can also boost your happiness.

- Happiness levels were shown to be greater among those who played recreational tennis compared to those who did not.

Science of Well-Being

Some individuals think that money can buy them happiness. However, several global studies have demonstrated that the quality of our interpersonal connections, rather than our material wealth, has a more significant impact on our happiness than either of these factors alone.

The term "well-being" refers to the degree to which an individual's life is satisfying to them, making it an important indicator for both individuals and broader social groups. The foundation of happiness is a stable environment in which to live and work. According to research, you may adopt the following five measures to better your mental health and overall well-being:

- **Staying connected:** Being social is making time for and investing in connections with people in your immediate and extended spheres of influence.
- **Being active:** Walking, swimming, cycling, and playing football are all great forms of exercise that can be enjoyed by almost everyone. There is mounting evidence that focusing on your physical health may also benefit your mental well-being.
- **Keep pursuing:** Acquiring new knowledge and abilities may do wonders for one's self-esteem and feeling of competence.

- **Being aware**: You may improve your outlook on life by increasing your awareness of the here and now, your surroundings, and your own emotions and ideas.

Happiness is the absence of unhappiness!

Blue-Zone Centenarians

Do you want to reach the age of 100?

The biggest populations of centenarians (people reaching age 100+) in the globe are found in the Blue Zones, which have been identified as 1) Ikaria, Greece; 2) Okinawa, Japan; 3) the Ogliastra Region of Sardinia; 4) Loma Linda, California; and 5) the Nicoya Peninsula of Costa Rica. They are surrounded by others who encourage them to make good choices. They're free to take some time to relax. They participate in groups, most often religious ones. They love their families very much, too.

Some Advice from Those Who Have Lived to be 100 from the "Blue Zone"

1. When you reach 80 percent fullness, it's time to call it a meal.
2. In the afternoon or evening, have your smallest meal of the day.
3. Stick to a plant-based diet, heavy on beans. Eat just 3 to 4 ounces of meat on rare occasions. On average, people living in the Blue Zone eat this a few times every month.
4. Consume alcohol on a regular basis, but in moderation (no more than two drinks each day).

5. People first: Blue zone centenarians prioritize their family and their communities. Keeping grandparents and great-grandparents close by or in the house is important for several reasons, including reducing the risk of illness and death for children.
6. Stress affects everyone, including those in "blue zones." All of the main age-related diseases are linked to chronic inflammation triggered by stress. What the world's oldest people have that we don't is a set of habits that help them deal with stress.
7. Both the Okinawans and the Nicoyans have a concept they term "why I wake up in the morning"; the Okinawans name it "Ikigai" and the Nicoyans call it "plan de vida." Having a clear understanding of your life's mission has been linked to a lifespan increase of up to seven years.
8. The folks who live the longest aren't the ones who join gyms, train for marathons, or pound the pavement. Instead, they are subjected to frequent environmental cues that encourage them to get up and move about without even realizing it. They cultivate gardens without the use of modern comforts like motorized instruments.

Right Mental Attitude

A healthy and right mental attitude is a powerful tool for making good changes in one's life. Looking on the bright side of the road can keep you happy and healthy even if things aren't always perfect.

Exercise and the right mental attitude are two sides of the same coin. They always go hand in hand. When you work out with other people, ideally, you are completing a difficult task together. This provides you with a feeling of shared success and collaboration, which in turn helps you to establish the correct mental attitude. You may cultivate a more pleasant mental attitude by meditating regularly and engaging in outdoor exercises such as jogging and brisk walking.

The Four Advantages of a Right Mental Attitude

- You'll have a better life if you try to see the glass as half full and approach each day with enthusiasm.
- A cheerful outlook raises energy levels, reduces stress, and protects against mental health issues like depression and stress.
- Positive thinking not only improves your quality of life, but it also opens doors to opportunities and the success you deserve.
- More vitality: Having a positive attitude constitutes one of the most valuable skills you can learn. Enhanced vitality, improved health, and increased potential for achievement.

Take-Home Messages

- Do not forget that happiness is key to healthy living.
- Always remember the **blue-zone centenarians.** Their life is filled with happiness and joy and there is no room for stress.
- Be watchful with your diet as your well-being depends on what you eat.

- Above all having the **right mental attitude** towards life is the only way to well-being and success.
- Exercise and happiness are very well linked, hence routine exercise is very important for happiness and to maintain the right mental attitude.

CHAPTER 11

Body Composition

Your body is a reflection of your lifestyle.

"Take care of your body. It's the only place you have to live." Jim Rohn

Various aspects of the human body may be measured and categorized for different therapeutic purposes. Carbon, calcium, potassium, and hydrogen are some examples of the atomic components of body composition; water, protein, and fat are examples of molecular components; extracellular fluid and body cell mass are examples of cellular components; and the amounts and distributions of adipose, skeletal, and muscle tissues are examples of tissue components.

Your hard work may not be showing up in the mirror yet, but that doesn't mean it isn't paying off. If you've been working out regularly, you could be seeing positive changes in your body composition. The scale can only tell you how much you weigh; it cannot identify the components of your body. A person's innate body type is established at birth by their skeletal framework and metabolic makeup. Most persons have characteristics of both the ectomorph and the mesomorph body types.

Typical Male Body Types

William H. Sheldon, a psychologist, first proposed the idea of somatotypes, or distinct body types, in the 1940s. Despite popular belief, this category is not exclusive to men and may be used to describe female anatomy as well. This categorizes bodies according to whether or not they are lean or have a hard time storing fat.

Ectomorphs: They usually do not have much muscle or fat on their bodies and are quite tall and thin. They struggle to put on weight. Examples of these people are fashion models and basketball players.

EndomorphS: Those that fit the description of "endomorph" tend to be stocky, muscular, and quick to put on weight. The endomorphic ideal is exemplified by Oprah Winfrey and Marilyn Monroe.

Mesomorphs: They are physically capable, athletic, and powerful people. They are of a healthy weight, neither overweight nor underweight, and may eat freely without health consequences. They are both able to acquire and lose weight with relative ease.

Regularly Occurring Female Forms

Females are more likely to be overweight. Their larger breasts, broader hips, bigger buttocks, and bigger thighs all contribute to a curvier physique. Each woman is an individual, however, there are a few distinct body types. Some typical forms are

Pear or Triangle: Those that fall into the pear or triangle category often have slimmer shoulders and hips than the average person.

The lower back, hips, and thighs often carry the bulk of a person's mass.

Inverted Triangle: If your upper body is larger than your lower, and your shoulders are broader than your hips, your body shape is an inverted triangle. This body type often puts on weight quickly and easily in the midsection and upper body. They also have wider shoulders and narrower hips than the average person.

Rectangle: If there is little to no difference between your waist and hips, your body shape is a rectangle. The hips and shoulders of a person with this body type are typically the same breadth.

Hourglass: The hourglass body shape is characterized by equal width at the shoulders and hips. This body type is characterized by a narrower waist in comparison to the bust and hips.

Oval or Apple: The Apple-shaped people have proportionally narrower upper and lower portions. People with this body type often have a thicker upper body and stomach but skinny legs.

The size and proportions of a body are affected by the individual's build. It's one of the things that makes each person unique. Some people have curvier bodies, while others have wider shoulders and greater muscle. After adolescence, most people have a fairly stable body type, however, this may shift depending on factors like nutrition, exercise, and other significant lifestyle and hormonal shifts. Similarly, some individuals have a hard time putting on weight, while others have a hard time shedding pounds.

What are the factors that determine body shape?

The form of a person's physique is influenced by several variables. Among them are: Genetics, age, sex, diet, and activity level.

A person's body contours may alter as a result of dietary and physical activity modifications. An ectomorph who wants to gain weight, for instance, may accomplish it with a healthy diet and regular exercise provided they are willing to put in the extra work.

Tips to Enhance Your Body Image

There are instances when people just don't like the way they look. A person with a highly curved figure may secretly wish they were more rectangular, whereas someone with a straight body may want curves. The notion of an "ideal body" form or type may put a lot of pressure on certain individuals, but the reality is that there is no such thing and that health is the most essential consideration regardless of appearance.

The National Eating Disorders Association suggests the following mental shifts for a healthier relationship with one's body:

- Take pride in your physical abilities.
- Keep in mind that appearances may be deceiving.
- Maintain a positive company.
- Stop talking to yourself negatively.
- Dress in a way that makes you feel good about yourself.
- Assess social media photos with caution.
- Everyone should remember that their physical appearance is simply one facet of their uniqueness and beauty.

Also, in the below table, I have provided workouts designed for different body shapes:

Table 11.1 Workout for body shapes

Body shape	Cardio workouts	Weight training
Apple	Three rounds of 50 walking lunges, a 200m jog, 20 box jumps, and 15 pull-ups. Sprinting, and rowing movements will also help. A cardio workout of at least 40-70 minutes, 3-5 times per week is desired. Apple-shaped women tend to carry more weight around their waistline, so it's important to perform core strengthening exercises like the plank as well as the side plank.	Strength training program composed of higher repetitions of at least 12-20 reps (with 30-60 sec of rest between the sets). Resistance exercise helps build and maintain muscle strength and promotes the growth of healthy muscle fibers. Exercise bands, free weights, and resistance machines can be used.
Banana	Outdoor sports of all kinds are excellent workouts. For example, swimming is perfect for this body type.	Glute exercises should be a big focus to get shape around the hips – deadlifts with weights, step-ups, and squats, which are all great for the lower body. Perform three sets of

		12 repetitions resting 45 to 60 seconds between each set.
Pear	Split squat with triceps extension, donkey kicks, jump squats, plank jumps, mountain climbers, and jump lunges. great for glutes, hips, and thighs!	Upper body, like triceps push-ups or biceps curls can be done. Perform the entire circuit 3 times, resting two minutes between each circuit. Perform each set of two exercises back-to-back.
Hourglass	Cardio for the upper body is swimming, rowing, and cross-country skiing. Cardio for the lower body is bicycling, walking, and running.	Though the goal here is to gain mass, it is important to use lightweight during resistance exercises, so as to not gain too much muscle mass. Biceps curls, shoulder presses, and squats can be done. The upper-body weight-training program to define muscles could include dips, lat pull-downs, tricep extensions, and bench presses.

Health experts and researchers talk about a person's "body composition," which is their total fat, water, bone, muscle, skin, and other lean tissue percentages. More information about your health may be gleaned by knowing your body composition. Even though individuals weigh the same, two persons might have vastly different requirements for health and fitness. The term "body composition" is used to describe how all of your bodily parts are classified. Fat mass and lean mass are the two most prevalent categories.

Body fat is collectively referred to as "fat mass." Muscles, organs, bones, and fluids all count towards the body's fat-free mass. It's possible that your weight won't shift if you make each of these adjustments simultaneously. In the first month of exercising, for instance, you could acquire two extra pounds of muscle. At the same time, if you increase your metabolic rate through exercise and dietary modifications, you may reduce your body fat percentage by two pounds. Your weight won't change since your fat-free mass grew by the same amount as your fat mass shrank.

Keeping a healthy body composition is often overlooked in favor of focusing on weight reduction. Checking your weight on a scale is a good way to get an idea of your overall weight, but it doesn't reveal anything about your body fat percentage or muscle mass. Fat mass and lean mass are the two main categories used to describe a person's body composition. Body fat percentage is a measure of fat mass. Body fat and lean mass are treated as separate entities in the two-component model of body composition.

By separating your total mass into fat mass and lean mass, a body composition study may provide you with a rapid assessment of your overall health. Accurately measuring a person's body composition provides detailed information that may be used to draw conclusions about their health and well-being. The amount of fat in a person's body varies more than anything else. Both types of fat are included in the overall quantity of body fat.

Normal physiological function depends on consuming enough essential fat. Essential fat includes the lipid-rich tissues found throughout the brain and spinal cord, as well as those found in the bone marrow, heart, lungs, liver, spleen, kidneys, intestines, and muscles. Whether it's the fat around your organs or in your midsection (visceral fat) or the "jiggly" fat just under your skin (subcutaneous fat), all of it is considered body fat (storage fat). Extra abdominal (or visceral) fat is associated with an increased risk of developing chronic diseases and other health problems.

Muscles, bones, ligaments, tendons, and internal organs all contribute to what's called "lean body mass." Fat-free mass and lean body mass are two different things. A little amount of vital fat is included in the lean body mass due to its presence in the bone marrow and other internal organs. However, the fat-free mass is calculated by estimating these necessary fat sources and subtracting them from the total body weight in the two-component model of body composition.

If someone starts working out with you, they could put on 1 kilogram of muscle in the first month. At the same time, people may be able to shed a pound or more of body fat by increasing their metabolic rate via exercise and dietary modifications. Since the increase in fat-free mass is equal to the reduction in fat mass, the individual's weight will remain constant.

Focusing on one's weight might lead to feelings of hopelessness and frustration that the program "isn't working." This is just one of many reasons why understanding your body composition rather than just your weight is so important. Body composition may be enhanced by the use of physical activity and exercise. They are essential for optimum muscular development and not just help you burn more calories.

Changing one's body composition may be as simple as cutting down on fat or bulking up on muscle. Fat reduction may be aided by a wide variety of exercises: When it comes to lowering abdominal adiposity, boosting lean body mass, and raising cardiorespiratory fitness, interventions that combine high-intensity aerobic and high-load strength training have the most positive benefits. These findings should be taken into account by clinicians when recommending exercise for individuals with obesity.

Why is it important?

Health risks may be better predicted by looking at a person's body composition and fat percentage rather than just their body mass index (BMI). An increased proportion of lean tissue and decreased percentage of body fat is indicative of a healthy body composition. Body composition is essential since it may offer you a better sense of your health risk. This is particularly true if you fall into the category of being overweight or obese according to your BMI because you have more muscle and lean tissue than other people in those categories. While shedding pounds and keeping an eye on the scale might be helpful, it cannot distinguish between fat reduction and muscle atrophy.

What are the different methods to measure body composition?

Body Mass Index

BMI is a tool that has been used by health professionals to assess body fatness and health. It's a mathematical equation that compares your weight to your height.

> BMI = (weight in pounds or kg)/(height squared) X 703
> For example (60 kg)/(154cm x 154cm) X 10,000 = 25.2

Below is a reference table:

Table 11.2: BMI

Less than 18.5	Underweight
18.5 to 24.9	healthy weight
25.0 to 29.9	Overweight
30 or higher	Obesity

You don't need any special equipment to measure BMI, making it a quick tool to assess body fat and health.

DEXA Scan

The whole-body DEXA scan is another option for measuring body fat. A DEXA scan is often used to evaluate bone density by doctors. It is also possible that it may be used in the process of determining body composition, such as the proportion of fat-free muscle mass to total muscle mass. When doing a DEXA scan, two beams of low-energy X-rays are used. Because of this, both soft tissue and bone may be seen in the picture. DEXA scans may also be preferred by doctors over underwater weighing for determining body fat percentage. Visceral fat, which is stored in the abdomen and around the organs, may also be estimated.

There are several variables that influence body fat percentages, such as sex, age, and body type. However, body fat levels may be a significant predictor of health since extremes in either direction are linked to a variety of health problems. The proportion of body fat you have is roughly estimated using a procedure called skinfold measuring. Calipers are used to measure the thickness of fat deposits at various locations around the body. Taking skinfold measurements is the first step in determining your body fat percentage. The number of formulae and computations is comparable to the number of methods for determining skinfold thickness. On the other hand, for your convenience, I have included a table that you can use as a handy reckoner to verify whether or not you are at the appropriate fat percentage, particularly for women.

Healthy Body Fat Percentage Chart

Table 11.3: Body fat percentage chart

Rating	20 - 39 years old	40 - 59 years old	60 - 79 years old
Low	<21 %	<23%	<24%
Healthy	21 - 33 %	23 - 35 %	24 - 36 %
Overweight	33 - 39 %	35 - 40 %	36 - 42 %
Obese	> 39 %	>40 %	>42 %

No matter what approach you use, it is essential to bear in mind that your weight will change on a regular basis. Because of this, the majority of body composition tests should only be used as a general reference point, and the results are most accurate when they are averaged over a certain period of time.

Ways to Improve Your Body Composition

You can enhance it by reducing the amount of body fat you have, increasing the amount of muscle you have, or doing both. Any one of these adjustments will result in a lower proportion of body fat, which is a single statistic that summarizes your whole body composition and may be lowered by making any of these modifications.

How do you improve your body composition?

1) Adopt an exercise plan that incorporates cardio along with weight training: Weight training builds muscle while cardiovascular exercise burns fat and glucose for fuel. Weight training is essential for everyone, especially ladies. As you become older, you lose muscle. Resistance exercise is the only proven method for regaining and gaining muscle mass. Therefore, you must include weight training in your routine.

2) Set realistic expectations: Setting reasonable goals is essential when beginning a fitness program. Getting in shape is a process, so be patient with yourself as you work towards your objectives. It's crucial to be realistic about how much time it may take to get a given appearance or certain outcomes. For instance, expecting to shed 5 kilograms in a single week is perhaps too ambitious. Instead, try focusing on a shorter time frame, such as a week or a month. For instance, if you want to lose weight, having a target of losing 1 kilogram every week is more realistic and maintainable.

3) Train with weights: One of the best strategies to reduce weight and enhance body composition is to lift weights. Including weight training in your regimen may boost your strength, muscle mass, and fat loss. Focusing on form and technique during weight training is crucial. It also matters what kind of weights you use. Because of the benefits of using many joints and muscles at once, free weights are frequently favored for strength training. Strengthen your arms by including bicep curls and triceps extensions in your routine, and your back by including pull-ups and chin-ups. Lifting the right amount of weight throughout your workouts is essential for muscular growth. Use a weight that makes it tough for you to complete more than 11 or 12 reps in a set. Perform at least 3–4 sets. Your muscles should feel like they've been exercised the day after the workout. Your attempts to gain muscle will only reach a plateau if you use the same weight each month.

4) Incorporate HIIT: Most individuals are fearful of pushing their limits while working out-perhaps of a sudden cardiac event or the sheer discomfort experienced due to breathlessness. If you want to change the shape of your body, High-Intensity Interval Training (HIIT) is the way to go. High-intensity interval training (HIIT) consists of short bursts of activity followed by recovery intervals. It's a fantastic method for maximizing your training time. Try to exhaust yourself during the high-intensity intervals so that you can recover fully during the low-intensity periods. If you want to improve your body composition and save time at the gym, HIIT is the way to go.

5) Sequence of exercise: Whenever possible, do your aerobic workouts first, and then go on to your weight training, if they fall on the same day. This will make EPOC (excess oxygen consumption after exercise) possible.

6) Get adequate sleep: One of the most crucial elements of optimizing your body composition and reducing weight is getting enough sleep. In addition to aiding in post-workout recovery, sleep also plays a role in stress management, hormone balance, and metabolic health.

7) Manage stress levels: Anxiety may play a significant role in sabotaging your efforts to improve your body composition. When we're under pressure, our bodies produce cortisol, which may make us less efficient at burning calories and more likely to keep them as fat.

8) Drink plenty of water: Water consumption is crucial for any health and fitness program. Staying hydrated with water will help you get the most out of your exercises and speed up the healing process afterward. Keeping hydrated also aids in temperature regulation, appetite suppression, and the digestive process.

9) Eat small, frequent meals rather than three large ones: According to one research, individuals who ate small, numerous meals per day ate fewer calories, ate more nutritious foods, and had a lower body mass index than those who ate fewer than four times in a 24-hour period.

10) To control and stabilize blood sugar, include protein at every meal: High-protein diets may also help individuals attain and maintain a healthy weight more successfully than moderate- or low-protein diets. It is an essential component found in meats, fish, and plant-based meals including nuts, beans, and legumes.

11) Do some exercise just before you eat: In what is known as a fasting state, it is often advised that you exercise first thing in the morning before eating breakfast. This is thought to aid with weight reduction. If necessary, schedule your pre-workout meal for around 90 minutes before your workout.

12) Consistency is the key: Your ability to adhere to or modify your exercise regimen is made simpler by the regularity of the habit. Being consistent with the good adjustments you make to your lifestyle can help you achieve your health and fitness objectives. Consistency in exercise is more important than occasional intense workouts for producing noticeable benefits.

Skinny Yet Fat

The phrase "skinny fat" describes a person who is underweight in terms of muscular mass but has a high proportion of body fat.

It's a widespread fallacy that having a tiny or slender body is a sign of excellent health, but this couldn't be farther from the truth. However, those who have a body mass index (BMI) that is within the "normal" range but have a greater percentage of body fat and a lower percentage of muscle mass may be at an increased risk of having the following conditions:

- Insulin resistance
- Poor cholesterol management
- Unhealthy levels of blood pressure

A person who is not physically fit is often characterized in a derogatory manner by the usage of this phrase. A person who is thought to be "skinny fat" may have a significant amount of visceral fat and little to no muscular definition. A higher risk of illnesses such as stroke and cardiovascular disease may be present in an individual who does not engage in regular physical activity and who consumes food that is not nutritionally enough. A person who has a metabolic profile that puts them at risk of developing metabolic illness is referred to as a "metabolically obese, normal weight" individual in the medical field. This describes someone who is thin but has a metabolic profile that puts them at risk.

I have included several dietary adjustments that I suggest you do in the following order to optimize your body composition:

- Reduce the number of simple carbs you consume and put more emphasis on obtaining the majority of your carbohydrates from whole grains, fruit, and vegetables.
- Make sure that your diet contains a sufficient amount of protein.
- Reduce your intake of sodas, alcoholic drinks, and juices, all of which are heavy in sugar and calories.
- Reduce your intake of added sugars as much as you can.
- Restrict yourself as much as possible from eating highly processed meals such as pastries, cereals with added sugar, and candy bars.
- After your workout, consume meals that are rich in protein.

Workout suggestions for various percentages of body fat are included below, broken down by both cardio and weight training.

Table 11.4 Suggested workout routine

Suggested workout routine	
Fat percentage level	**Cardio**
Normal	Aerobic exercise like walking, running, swimming, and/or cycling. On average, bi-weekly strength training sessions can also help you in getting a toned body. This can be done 3 - 4 times a week.
High	Extending the duration (4 - 5 times a week) of the above-mentioned activities can help shed some calories.
Weight training irrespective of body fat percentage	
Focusing on the upper and lower body • At least exercise 6 days per week • Up to 30–50 minutes per day • 5–10 reps/exercise • 2–3 body parts/day	

When you put in the effort to maintain a healthy lifestyle by working out and eating well but see no change in the number that appears on the scale, it may be quite disheartening. However, just because you haven't seen any changes in your weight, it doesn't indicate that all of your efforts have been in vain. Your body composition may be changing for the better, particularly if you are engaging in physical activity.

CHAPTER 12

Fat but Fit Paradox

Can you be overweight and healthy?

The perception that having a healthy weight corresponds to having a normal weight is widespread, yet there is a possibility that this assumption is incorrect. Persons of normal weight who are not physically fit have a much greater risk of death from all causes combined, as well as cardiovascular disease, than persons of normal weight who are physically fit. In addition, some readers may find even more fascinating the fact that some studies have shown that people who are of normal weight but unfit might be at a higer risk than those who are obese but fit, which may appear contradictory.

When compared with their colleagues who are also obese but not physically active, those who are overweight but fit have a risk of depression that is 50%lower. Although being overweight raises a person's risk of being susceptible to a variety of health problems, including heart disease, stroke, diabetes, and some cancers, numerous studies have demonstrated that a person's illness risk is connected not to weight, but rather to body fat and where it's distributed in the body. This is the case even if being overweight raises a person's risk of these problems. Your fitness will increase regardless of your weight if you exercise on a regular basis.

Nevertheless, a study has shown that one cannot be 'fat but healthy. According to the author of the research and a professor of exercise physiology at the European University of Madrid, Alejandro Lucia, "the detrimental health effects of excess body fat are not likely to be eliminated by the beneficial effects of regularly engaging in physical activity." Therefore, it is important for everyone, regardless of how much they weigh, to engage in physical activity in order to protect their health. This brings to mind a real-life occurrence that I came across while pursuing a career path in a related field.

> During my days of practice, I came across very special lady named Kiara who weighed 115 kg. She was 5.5 feet tall and was in a very bad condition when I first encountered her. But she was so strong-hearted that she never expressed her problems to the outside world. But during our very first conversation, she broke down with tears and started sharing her story with me. She said that she underwent a very difficult phase in her marriage, and she got separated. When I asked her about her kids, she said she has one daughter, and she's looking after her as a single parent. She expressed both the physical and emotional stress that she was going through. She said she tried many different diet regimes to shed her weight, and she did lose a few kilos by practicing some very bad diet protocol, but the moment she stopped the diet she regained all the weight, back which led her towards depressive episodes.
>
> But under my guidance, she started working out and promised herself that this time she would never lose confidence in her body until she was satisfied. Eventually, she found it very difficult to cope with the exercises, felt breathless and tired,

started to lose her confidence level, and wasn't enjoying her journey of weight loss. But gradually, over a span of 6 -7 months, she started loving the journey and regained her confidence. She lost almost 18 kg and her body started healing with becoming more flexible and stronger. However, she found it difficult to maintain her weight within the normal range. But due to her stability and focus on her well-being, she was soon able to walk comfortably and involved herself in different body-training workouts including yoga, and started inspiring other overweight women as well. We were all happy with her performance, and she considered herself fat but fit. The exercise was much easier for her now than before. She aimed to bring her fat percentage down to 20.

Also, as per my instructions, she has modified her daily activities accordingly such as:

- She makes up her mind to do all the household chores by herself.
- She has completely stopped consuming junk food instead she has started preparing food by herself.
- Whenever possible she goes shopping on a walk.
- She continues her exercise and sometimes even plays music and starts dancing which can give her mental and physical stability.
- She engages herself in some outdoor games with her daughter.

CHAPTER 13

Fitness on the Go

Fitness on the Go: Achieve Health Anywhere, Anytime

Maintaining your mental and physical health doesn't have to seem like an enormous challenge if you divide your goals into smaller, more achievable chunks. Being a working individual is challenging in and of itself. It's challenging for women to prioritize their health when they are occupied with other responsibilities at the same time, such as raising children and maintaining a career. What women need to know is that their bodies require additional fuel and care to keep up with all the extra work they're putting in.

While a nutritious diet is certainly helpful, it's not enough to maintain a healthy lifestyle. If you want to maintain your health and vitality, you must work out regularly. In addition to assisting with weight control, it also improves general health. It's also important to keep up with your regular exercise routine when on the road for business. Work trips away from home may be nerve-wracking and full of surprises. A rigorous conference schedule, bad weather, or an unreasonable customer might put you in a spot. How are you supposed to maintain a serious workout schedule on top of everything else?

Negative patterns of behavior that develop while on business travel may have a significant influence on both your own well-being and the effectiveness of your trip. It's tempting to treat business travels as "cheat days" and slack off on your usual exercise and nutrition routine, but in reality, you'll be far more productive if you find some way to stay active during your trip.

So, what should be done? Whatever the case may be, doing nothing is most definitely not the best course of action.

Thankfully, there are novel ways to get in shape for busy professionals than just hitting the gym at their hotel. I've included my five best recommendations for staying in shape even while traveling.

1. Stay Active While You Commute

Light physical exercise during the commute may help counteract the negative effects of sitting for lengthy periods of time and provide the busy person with some structure to their fitness program. Those who know they will have a stopover at the airport, for instance, should bring running shoes and use the time to get some exercise. Whenever possible, use the stairs instead of the lift for even more straightforward problem-solving. Check to see if there is a gym or group exercise class close to the airport, or if there is time, engage in a fast workout or jog around the nearby park.

2. Start right Away

After a lengthy car trip, plane voyage, or train excursion, it might be tough to find the drive to do anything other than rest after you've finally arrived at your destination. You may make things simpler for yourself by stowing your workout attire in a piece of baggage that is easily accessible, such as a carry-on bag, or by donning them during your commute if you have the option to do so. In this manner, as soon as you reach your location, you will already be dressed and prepared to begin your workout.

3. Take care of your Body

It's easy to lose sight of the fact that the same rules apply when you're not in your usual setting. Maintaining an active lifestyle calls for a fitness-ready diet. Even while on the road, it's important to maintain a healthy routine of eating, drinking lots of water, and getting enough sleep. Whenever possible, stock up on goods to reduce the pressure to eat out at every meal. In addition to walking, you may substitute a high-quality meal replacement drink, such as a bulk gainer or protein smoothie, for one of your regular meals.

4. Take a walk after unch

After lunch, going for a stroll is beneficial if you want to avoid feeling lethargic in the afternoon. To maintain your level of energy and concentration throughout the afternoon, try going for a stroll around the office during your lunch break. These short, easy walks can not only keep you exercising but also have the potential to lift your spirits.

5. Basic Workout You Can Do Anywhere

Starting off with activities like biking, hiking, and walking tours is a GREAT way to get your body in shape, but I'm sure you already knew that. It's a kind of exercise that doesn't feel like exercise since you get to see new places.

There are four aspects of fitness that must be prioritized if you want to reach your fitness goals. If you don't put these four pillars into motion, you'll never reach your full potential. Let's examine some of the many options for maintaining the four cornerstones of fitness while on the road.

Cardio

Explore your destination on foot before deciding what to do there. The act of sightseeing itself may be a kind of exercise. Logging your daily activity is a breeze. If you're on the road for an extended period of time, the time spent waiting around might sap your motivation. You have a goal in mind, you're carrying a backpack, and it's difficult to locate nutritious meals. Nonetheless, if you find yourself with a 30-minute stopover, get up and stretch your legs. You can work out the kinks in your body that developed from sitting for too long on the trip, and you'll feel much better for it.

Strength

Planks are one of the most well-known and simple workouts because of their ability to strengthen and tone several of the body's major muscle groups simultaneously. Try three sets of five 30- to 60-second planks in your hotel room to discover how this easy workout may benefit your body when you're away from home. Make the most of the hotel's facilities if you're going to stay there. You may get some exercise by walking about the neighborhood or by making use of the fitness center's swimming pool, cardio machines, and weights.

Flexibility

Here are some easy, fundamental exercises you may perform whenever you have a few minutes to spare and want to get some exercise and maintain your flexibility. When waiting in line for meals, at an event, at the bank, or when serving as a chaperone or working the front desk, you may find yourself on your feet for long periods of time. Here are a few ways you may incorporate these easy stretches into your regular routine.

- Heels off the ground
- Bending at the waist
- Rolling the shoulders, stretching the hamstrings, etc.

Endurance

Without causing unnecessary stress or a decline in fitness, training may be easily included in travel for both pleasure and business. Here are some suggestions about how to approach travel with a spirit of perseverance.

Hiking: When you hike, you burn more calories and build greater stamina because of the increase in height.

Running: Accept the challenge and look for opportunities to go for a stroll, no matter where you are. Embrace the run.

Incorporate training into vacations for work or pleasure by renting a bike to ride around town or the countryside, going for a run along a beautiful route, or swimming in a local lake.

Major health issues due to inactivity

Prolonged inactivity, whether seated or lying down, raises the probability that you may develop serious health issues later in life. As with physical health, mental health may suffer from excessive sitting. If you stay still for too long, a blood clot may form in your legs, a condition known as deep vein thrombosis (DVT). When traveling a long distance or when bedridden due to an illness or injury, for instance, you may not be able to move about as much as usual which can ultimately result in DVT.

Pack right while traveling!

- **Attire:** Pack your workout clothes as the first step. One is all that is required. Pick out some exercise clothing that won't weigh you down, can be hand washed in the sink, and will be dry by morning. Also, don't forget to take your athletic footwear, sport or running shoes.
- **Yoga Mat:** Pack a lightweight yoga mat that weighs just two pounds and can be easily foded into a small square.
- **Resistance Band:** Obviously, you don't want to bring weights, but a resistance band is very versatile as it can let you complete a plethora of strength workouts without taking up too much space in your bag.

Working out while on vacation is a great idea. Whether you're traveling for work or pleasure, switching up your usual routine may help you discover exciting new methods to get your heart rate up, have some laughs, and maintain your fitness level.

CHAPTER 14

Posture: The New Beauty Standard

Posture: The Foundation of Health, Confidence, and Beauty

Your general health and even appeal depends on having a good posture, which has several advantages such as less back discomfort, more energy, and more self-assurance.

Having a proper posture may help you prevent muscular strain, soreness, exhaustion, and many other common illnesses and medical disorders, which are crucial for your general health and to avoid faulty body maintainacne. Even if your posture is a contributing factor to one or more health issues, it's never too late to adjust or improve it.

What are the advantages of a proper posture?

Numerous health benefits of having excellent posture include both physical and psychological benefits:

Decreased Back Pain

Over 25% of working people have low back discomfort annually, with poor posture ranking among the top risk factors. Long durations of slouching may place too much strain on the discs, ligaments, and muscles in the spine, resulting in low back discomfort. Even while you're sitting down, maintaining excellent posture may significantly lower your chance of experiencing back discomfort.

Decreased Headaches

Headaches are often brought on by stress in the neck and upper back muscles as a result of poor posture. The most typical sort of headache is a tension headache, which is characterized by pressure, tightness, and dull, throbbing pain in the forehead, neck, or back of the head. Tension headaches are often helped by yoga and stretching, but fixing improper posture may permanently end chronic headaches.

Enhanced Lung Function

Poor posture and slouching may compress the lungs, resulting in a labored breathing and diminished respiratory function. Maintaining proper posture may often expand your lung's capacity to facilitate breathing. Walking, jogging, and swimming may all become simpler cardio workouts as a result of better breathing and excellent posture.

Higher Levels of Energy

Having a poor posture may make you feel exhausted and low on energy because it restricts blood flow and misaligns bones and joints. For oxygen and nutrients to reach your cells, where they would be utilized for energy, proper blood circulation is required. Bones and joints that are in proper alignment support good muscular function, which may make you feel more energized and less exhausted.

Improved Form during Exercise

You can exercise with perfect form if you have good posture, which lowers your chance of getting hurt. For instance, squatting while hunching over or arching your back increases the chance of developing persistent lower back discomfort. If your posture and alignment are correctly established, your physical improvements and exercise outcomes will also be easier to achieve and more obvious.

Enhanced Confidence

Having excellent posture may influence your confidence and how you feel about your looks, both directly and indirectly. For instance, having excellent posture may increase your energy and motivate you to be more sociable and active.

Additionally, having a good posture may give you a taller, slimmer, and more toned appearance. According to a research, having an excellent posture might help women who are unhappy with their bodies to feel better about themselves and boost their confidence.

What does having a good posture mean?

In order to have a good posture, you should always make sure that your body is symmetrically positioned, particularly while sitting, standing, and lying down. Many individuals naturally have excellent posture, however, certain lifestyle choices and habits may over time alter posture. For instance, persons who spend a lot of time leaning forward in their seats while using a computer or playing video games may be more susceptible to developing poor posture.

Here are some tips for maintaining proper posture while standing, sitting, and lying down:

Sitting

To keep your feet from hanging in the air, place them flat on the floor or on a footrest. Try not to sit with your legs crossed and keep your ankles in front of your knees. Keep your knees at hip level or below the hips and away from the chair's edge. Make sure the chair hat you're on adequately supports your middle and lower back, and relax your shoulders.

Fig 14. 1 Proper sitting posture

Standing

Maintain a straight back as you stand up to your maximum height. Imagine someone dragging you up towards the ceiling by the top of your head to make sure you're doing it right. Maintain a tiny bend in your knees and avoid locking them.

Keep your core muscles engaged while letting your arms hang freely and tucking your tummy in. Put your feet shoulder-width apart and gently shift your weight from your heels to the front of your feet. Try not to tilt your head back, forward, or to the side; just keep it level.

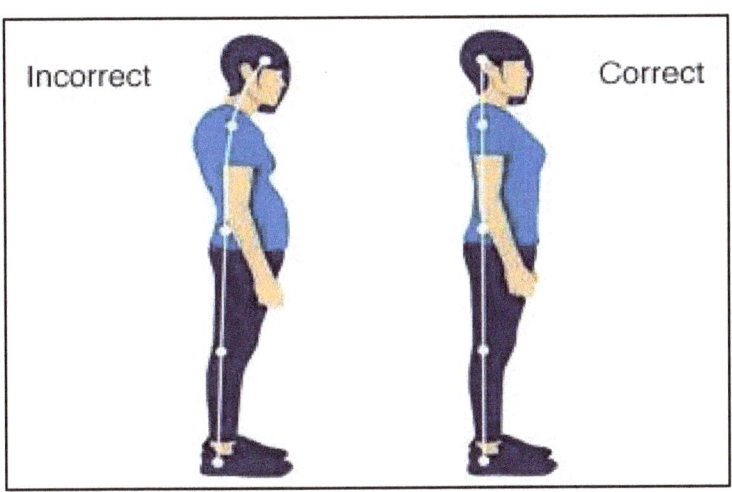

Fig 14.2 Proper standing posture

Source: Mayo Foundation for Medical Education and Research

Lying Down

The greatest position to guarantee a proper posture is often lying on your side since it relieves strain on your back. To correct your spine if side sleeping is painful for you, consider putting a cushion between your knees.

Avoid sleeping on your stomach since it may make the discomfort in your back worse. Additionally, depending on your posture, weight, and any current sleep issues, your doctor may provide you with an advice on how to discover the ideal sleeping position for you.

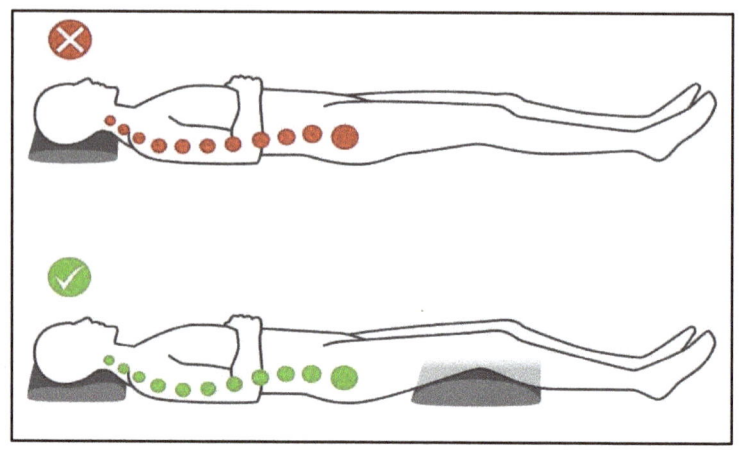

Fig 14.3 Proper sleeping posture

Source: Foothills Sports Medicine Physical Therapy

What can I do to correct my posture?

You may gradually improve your posture by engaging in certain behaviors and routines until it becomes more natural. Here are some suggestions to help you stand more upright.

- Start consistently exercising since it may strengthen your bones and muscles, lessen pain naturally, and stabilize your spine. Watch instructional videos or work with a fitness professional if you need assistance learning the right forms and techniques.

- Make sure your desk is ergonomic to protect your back and avoid stress headaches. Follow the instructions that come with your office desk or chair to set them up in the ergonomic positions that are most comfortable for you. Place your computer display squarely in front of your face.

- Spending too much time bending down, which may put additional strain on the spine, should be avoided.

Rearrange your furniture so that everything is within reach and you aren't leaning over too much.
- To prevent slouching when relaxing on seats and sofas at home, prop oneself up using cushions.
- Change your attire to promote good posture and prevent back discomfort and slouching. Consider purchasing a rucksack that you can put over both shoulders if you often carry heavy stuff in a purse or shoulder bag to lessen the pressure on your shoulders, neck, and back.

A healthy posture improves your beauty!

Individuals who are physically appealing are often in good health and have symmetrical features.

A balance created by having good posture—holding the head, shoulders, and trunk in ideal alignment—allows our many physiological systems to operate at their peak. Chronic imbalances may occur from this, which may cause discomfort. Additionally, studies from the 19th century reveal that our posture has an impact on our mood, vitality, and self-confidence, all of which have an impact on how attractive we look to others. Supermodels, A-list actresses, and the rest of the "beautiful people" are never seen slumped over as they go down the red carpet or down the runway.

Excellent posture begins in early childhood!

Adults often worry about back issues, which are also becoming more prevalent in kids and teenagers. Poor posture, which may include slouching, rounding of the shoulders and neck, or too dramatic arching or hunching of the back, is a significant contributing cause in kids. Your spine, ligaments, tendons, and muscles are subjected to a tremendous amount of strain and wear and tear in these situations.

While everyone may benefit from proper posture, children need to be particularly mindful of it. Early development of good habits in children increases their likelihood of continuing to practice them as adults, which reduces the likelihood of back issues and other troubles as they age.

What does proper posture look like?

Did someone ever advise you to "stand up straight!" when you were a child? That, in a nutshell, is a proper posture. When standing, your shoulders should be directly above your hips, your weight should be distributed evenly across your feet, and your chin should be parallel to the floor. Rolling your shoulders up, back, then down can help you visualize how it feels. You may also see a straight line passing through your ear, shoulder, and hip, perpendicular to your side and parallel to the floor.

The same rule applies while sitting; try to maintain a tall, upright posture rather than slouching. To ease pressure on your tailbone when you sit down, lean forward, slide your bottom to the back of the chair, and then sit up.

Maintaining a straight posture will be easier if you relax your shoulder muscles and engage your core abdominal muscles. In addition to strengthening muscles, increasing breathing efficiency, reducing chronic discomfort, and making one seem more self-assured and robust, good posture provides many of the same advantages as exercise.

How to Teach Good Posture to Children

There is no fast treatment for poor posture, and nagging your children typically doesn't help either. Making excellent posture a daily habit requires guidance, gentle coaching, plenty of practice, and setting a good example early on.

Children should avoid spending too much time sitting down and gain at least one hour of strenuous activity every day. Exercises like yoga and pilates, which encourage strength, flexibility, and balance, may greatly improve posture. Modern living involves some screen time, but there are ways to limit it, take more breaks, and raise the device to eye level.

The way people interact has been made easier and more comfortable by smartphones, computers, and other digital devices; yet, these technological tools have also led to the emergence of a new physical ailment known as "**text neck**" syndrome, which causes discomfort in the neck and shoulders. Particularly in the wake of the COVID-19 epidemic, lengthy periods of poor posture and excessive usage of these gadgets are causing severe health problems in kids and teens as well.

This medical disorder describes the beginning of a *cervical spine degeneration* brought on by the recurrent strain of often bending our heads forward while we stare down at our phones or when we "text" for extended periods of time. Teenagers are more likely to develop text neck syndrome because they are more likely than ever to slouch over cellphones and laptops for extended periods of time, sometimes for several hours each day and several days a year. Text neck syndrome is a common health problem among adults, according to the National Library of Medicine. However, the new research indicates that the prevalence of the condition has shifted from adults to children of all ages.

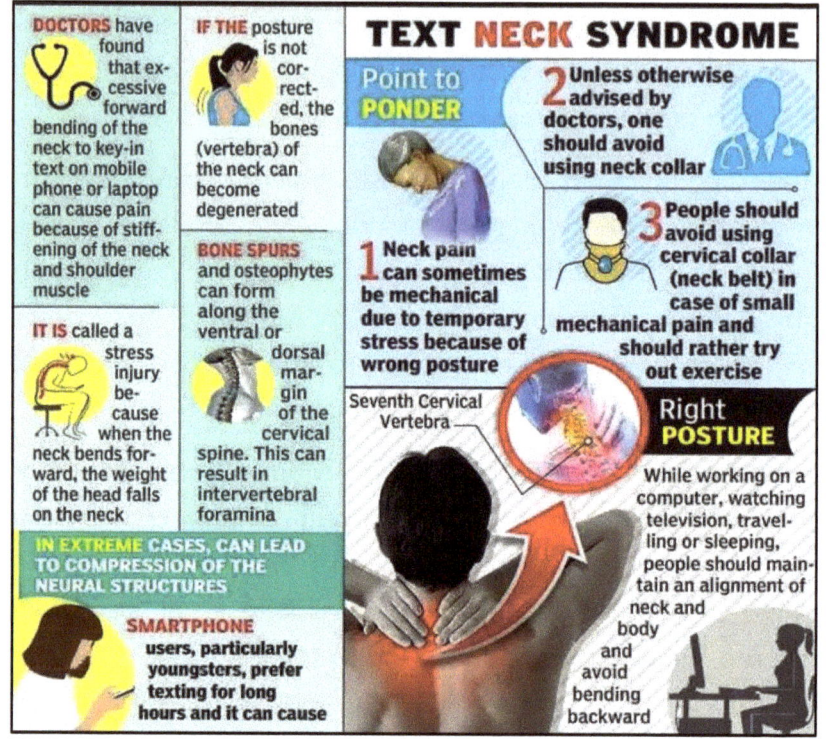

Fig 14. 4 Depiction of text neck syndrome and its prevention

The majority of children also experience *kyphosis* as a concern. It's a curvature in the neck and upper back that isn't normal. Children with kyphosis seem rounded or "hunchbacked." Although certain instances of *kyphosis* are present from birth, the majority occur in adolescence.

A healthy and normal curvature in the spine's front-to-back direction is present. However, a pediatric spine expert should be seen if a kid has a forward bend of the spine of 50 degrees or more.

Adolescent _kyphosis_ is often minor. A doctor should keep a careful eye on an adolescent with kyphosis until they have finished growing. Many won't need medical attention. Severe forward curves may cause discomfort and deformities that can compress the lungs and make breathing difficult. The only way to treat severe kyphosis is by bracing, which may possibly include surgery.

What are the symptoms of kyphosis?

- Visible hump, typically in the upper back
- Upper back appearing higher than normal when bending forward
- Head always or almost always bent forward
- Excessive rounding of the shoulders

Aggressive therapy is not necessary for most children with postural and Scheuermann's kyphosis. Physical therapy, bracing, and observation and monitoring might all be part of their treatment.

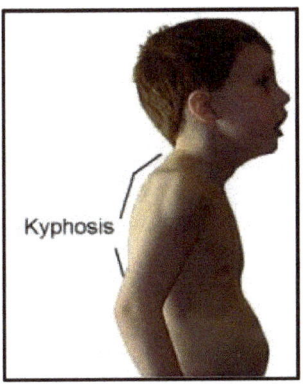

Fig 14. 5: A child with kyphosis

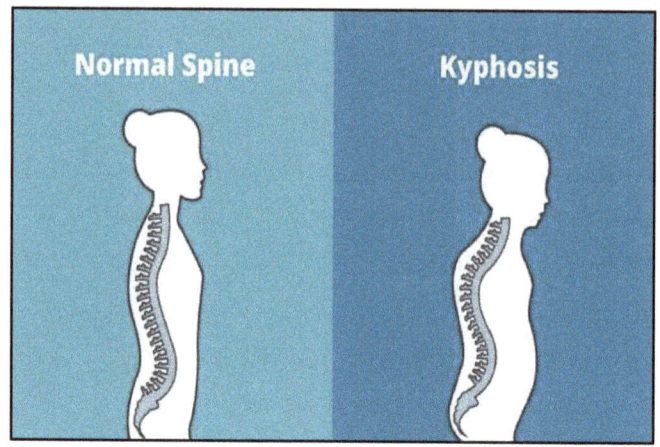

Figure 14.6 Normal spine and spine with kyphosis

Assure your kids that they are wearing their backpacks correctly and that the burden shouldn't exceed 10% of their body weight.

Although practicing proper posture from children requires dedication, the long-term rewards—fewer injuries, a lower chance of developing chronic pain, and enhanced breathing, mood, and self-assurance—are well worth it.

Take-Home Messages!

- Health is important! Therefore, developing proper posture during childhood might be advantageous as an adult.
- Educate children about good posture.
- To maintain balance, it's vital to stand up straight and place your weight over your feet. This may assist you in overcoming many disabilities.

CHAPTER 15

Putting It All Together

As the chapter name suggests, I have tried to put it all together that we have learnt in the book to improve our health span from the early years of life through various exercise regimes. As we age, the fundamental structure of our bodies remains remarkably constant. We all share the same basic physical components, including six joints, one spine, one heart, one liver, and two kidneys. What has significantly evolved over time is our life. Positive changes in our way of living can have a profound impact on both our life and health in cohesion.

The 3 Principles of Exercising Right

To optimize our health and longevity, it's essential to adhere to the three core principles of effective exercise:

1. Stretching of muscles

2. Mobility of joints

3. Strengthening of muscles and endurance

Remember, there is always a bridge between action indicating proactivity here and inaction. Once you embark on your fitness journey and consistently try to cross that bridge, the path becomes smoother and more rewarding.

Major and Minor Pillars of Fitness

Attaining comprehensive fitness comprises four major pillars, which are further complemented by six minor pillars. This inclusive strategy guarantees a diverse fitness routine, fostering overall health and enhancing performance.

Table 15.1 Major and minor pillars of fitness

4 Major Pillars of Fitness	Example
Cardio	*Running, swimming, and cycling*
Strength	*Weightlifting, resistance training*
Endurance	*High-repetition weight training, bodyweight exercises*
Flexibility	*Stretching exercises, and yoga*
6 Minor Pillars of Fitness	**Example**
Balance	*Single-leg exercises, stability exercises*
Coordination	*Agility drills, sport-specific drill*
Power	*Plyometric exercises, Olympic weightlifting*
Reflexes	*Cone drills, ladder drills*
Reaction Time	*Reflex training, sport-specific drills*
Speed	*Sprinting, interval training*

You may be interested in incorporating cardio, or maybe even weight training, stretches, or yoga into your routine. Imagine yourself in workout attire all day, seeking to seamlessly blend everything. However, this is not the reality. The commitment of time and effort for different fitness components varies depending on your individual needs. To enhance your workout routine, consider the following:

1. Address your specific requirements.

2. Practice mindful exercise.

3. Emphasize overall well-being.

4. Adopt a balanced diet plan and adjust as needed.

5. Address other factors like stress, sleep, and your overall perspective on exercise and life.

Addressing Your Individual Needs

Everyone possesses unique characteristics, and their fitness requirements differ accordingly. Most individuals benefit from incorporating cardio, weight training, flexibility exercises, sufficient rest, and a balanced nutrition plan. Evaluate the following aspects:

- Determine the appropriate amount of cardio on the basis of your physiology..
- Establish a suitable weight training regimen based on your goals.
- Explore methods to enhance flexibility in your fitness routine.
- Identify the optimal amount of sleep for your overall well-being.
- Define a well-balanced diet that aligns with your nutritional needs.
- Clarify specific fitness goals you aim to achieve.

These pivotal questions necessitate personalized responses. Individuals should define their own fitness objectives and design customized routines that fit their goals and lifestyles. Consulting with a fitness professional is often recommended for tailored guidance.

The 5 Basic Rules of Exercising Right

Now let's delve into the five fundamental rules that apply to any exercise program, whether you're a beginner or an expert:

Rule 1: Mindset: *Focus on what you want to do and train the mind to achieve it.*

Your mindset plays a pivotal role in your fitness journey. To achieve your goals, focus on what you want to accomplish and train your mind accordingly. A successful mindset involves the right attitude, temperament, realistic thinking, and a willingness to adapt and improve. Embracing a positive attitude towards ageing, known as a "healthy ageing mindset," can significantly impact your approach to growing older gracefully with the right mental attitude and maintaining your health. The major part of anti-ageing is exercising smartly.

Rule 2: Consistency: *Do a little more every time and stay regular.*

Consistently push your boundaries and aim to do a little more every time you exercise. Strive to excel and make every day a step toward achieving your best.

Rule 3 : Motivation: *Keep the motivation high to achieve results.*

Set achievable goals and gradually work towards long-term objectives. Motivation is what gets you started, and habits are what keep you going. Self-Determination Theory (SDT) emphasizes the importance of getting started and cultivating the motivation needed to maintain your fitness routine and feel good.

Rule 4 :Adaptation: *The body gets used to what you do. So, stretch the limits.*

Our body adapts to the challenges you present. Take one task at a time and master it through consistent practice. Whether it's walking every morning or aiming for 10,000 steps a day, gradually increase the intensity of your exercise to reap the benefits.

Rule 5 :Rest and Recovery*: Take enough rest to heal, and recover, which makes you stronger, fitter and healthier.*

In between exercise sessions, prioritize rest and recovery to allow your body to heal and become stronger, fitter, and healthier. This encompasses hydration, nutrition, posture, temperature management, and stress management. Adequate rest is essential to cater to your body's physical, mental, emotional, and sensory needs.

Keeping Holistic Health in Mind

Setting out on a fitness journey today presents unique challenges due to the widespread availability of products like fat burners, protein supplements, amino acids, and creatinine. Consumers are inundated with options that, while not necessarily essential, promise remarkable performance improvements and a sculpted physique. There are several individuals being persuaded to adopt these unnecessary supplements, despite their high costs, with promises of expedited and enhanced goal achievement.

Holistic healthcare involves a thorough approach that considers all aspects of an individual —their mental, spiritual, emotional, and physical well-being. The main objective is not to just treat symptoms but to explore and tackle the root causes of health issues. A holistic approach is crucial for achieving effective rehabilitation.

Holistic health should take precedence. Research suggests that an excessive intake of protein and reliance on fat burners can pose serious health risks. The pursuit of fitness should not compromise long-term health and well-being. Consider the paradox of pursuing a 38-cm biceps or a 53-cm waist if it results in kidney failure.

The safety of fat burners remains uncertain, given their potential to raise metabolic rates, induce undue increases in heart rate, and even trigger fatal irregular heart rhythms. Even when labelled as herbal, caution is necessary, as this designation does not ensure safety. Many individuals commit to fat burners without fully comprehending the potential long-term consequences.

Reflect on whether it's worthwhile to compromise your life and health for a marginal reduction in waist size. Unfortunately, for some, the allure proves irresistible. While supplements have their place, it's crucial to assess whether you genuinely need them. Consider whether a protein supplement is necessary or if your diet already provides sufficient protein.

Resist the allure of advertising, the latest trends, or the enthusiasm of an overzealous trainer. Promises of rapid results in advertisements often employ clever marketing strategies to attract unsuspecting customers. Learn to respect your body and refrain from subjecting it to abuse based on momentary attractions. Fitness is a gradual process, and prioritizing long-term health over short-term gains is essential.

How do we address other issues such as stress, sleep, and attitudes towards exercise and life in general?

The dynamic relationship between stress and sleep holds significant importance in the journey of weight loss and achieving optimal fitness. If you face difficulties with stress levels or sleep patterns, it is recommended that you seek guidance from a professional. As highlighted earlier, nurturing the right mindset towards fitness is paramount. Although the path may not always be smooth, adopting a positive perspective can enhance its enjoyability. It is crucial to dispel misconceptions and dismantle myths surrounding fitness and diet that could hinder your progress and obstruct the way to attaining a fit and healthy body.

Knowing Cognitive Behavioral Therapy (CBT)

This psychological intervention entails guiding the patient in shifting their mindset from negative to positive. Studies show that Cognitive Behavioral Therapy (CBT) can be a valuable tool, especially when integrated with diet and exercise, to support weight loss. Weight gain and the struggles in weight loss often involve psychological elements such as stress, anger, negative thoughts, and depression. Psychological intervention, specifically through CBT sessions, proves beneficial in addressing these issues. Clients engage in sessions to understand the thought processes that impede success and receive coaching to reshape their thinking for effective weight loss.

Evaluate your commitment to long-term success rather than opting for a quick weight loss. Despite potential challenges in the journey, the sustained effort promises ultimate rewards. For a thorough assessment, consider baseline blood tests to examine blood sugar, hemoglobin, cholesterol, and thyroid profile. Additionally, monitor blood pressure and vital signs, and if necessary, undergo a stress test.

Undergoing a Fitness Assessment

A thorough fitness assessment should cover the following:

1. Measuring height, weight, body fat percentage, blood pressure, and pulse.

2. Documenting girth measurements at various points.

3. Assessing cardiovascular endurance, strength, and flexibility using suitable tests.

Table 15.2 Sample tests

Fitness Parameter	Sample Tests
Cardiovascular Fitness	1-mile walk test
	1.5-mile run test
	Step test
	Swim test
Strength	1 rep max
	12 rep max for various major muscles like the shoulders, chest, back, legs, etc.
	Core strength
Flexibility	Sit-and-reach test
	Shoulder rotation test
Body Composition	Girth circumferences
	Body fat percentage
	Weight on scale
	BMI
	Waist hip ratio

The fitness assessment is not meant to pass a judgment or, worse, ridicule your current size or health status. It serves as a baseline evaluation, offering a starting point for you to work towards improving your health and fitness. Without establishing these baseline values, it becomes challenging to measure progress.

For example, in your initial fitness assessment, let's assume you complete the 1-mile walk test in 19 minutes. While this might initially appear as a significant duration, it's important not to perceive it negatively. After a month of dedicated training, if your reassessment reveals an improved time of 14 minutes for the 1-mile walk, it signifies remarkable progress in cardiovascular fitness, even if weight loss may not be substantial. Acknowledging such improvements can be highly motivating, especially for individuals who may not experience rapid weight loss and could otherwise feel disheartened.

Setting your Goals

To establish effective fitness goals, engage in goal-setting with a qualified professional. Ensure your goals are S.M.A.R.T.

S-Specific: Clearly define your objective, such as "losing 2 kg in 3 weeks," rather than a vague "losing weight."

M-Measurable: Use quantifiable metrics like waist circumference or fat percentage for tangible and measurable progress. For example, "losing 2 cm around my waist" is measurable, while "becoming slim around my waist" is not.

A-Attainable: Set realistic goals to avoid frustration and failure. For instance, "losing 20 kg in 2 months" may be lofty and potentially unhealthy; consider practicality and health implications.

R-Realistic: Be practical about your approach, considering your lifestyle, family, and work commitments. Overcommitting can lead to setbacks and hinder progress.

T-Time-Bound: Establish a specific timeframe for your goal to avoid a vague and unproductive fitness routine.

Embarking on a fitness journey involves various adjustments. Food management takes time to adapt, and there may be fluctuations between healthy and less healthy eating days.

Overcoming excuses and maintaining consistency are crucial for sustained progress.

Recommendations for Your Approach to Fitness Goals

A successful exercise strategy is essential for managing fitness efficiently, striving for optimal results while minimizing time commitment and the potential for injury. The suggestions provided in the table below are general and may require modifications based on individual variations. For example, if time constraints exist, one could explore combining weight training with cardio in a High-Intensity Interval Training (HIIT) routine.

Table 15.3 Fitness recommendations

My Goal	Cardio	Weight Training	Flexibility	Nutrition	Rest
Fat Loss	45 minutes x 6 days a week. Moderate intensity. Borg scale 5-6.	Perform a total body workout twice weekly using a circuit or super-set format, minimizing rest between exercises to keep the heart rate elevated.	Stretch every day for about 10 minutes.	Total calorie intake approximately 15 per cent less than your actual calorie requirement.	6-8 hours

Muscle Gain	20 minutes x 4 times a week. High Intensity. Borg scale 6-8.	Every day-1 to 2 body parts/day. At least 3 exercises per body part; 5-8 sets per exercise. Do the exercises slowly and rest for about a minute between sets.	Every day 15 minutes.	Total calorie intake approximately 15 per cent more than your actually requirement. Protein requirement of 30 per cent of your total calorie intake.	Minimum 7-8 hours
Stress Relief	30 Minutes x 6 days a week. Lower intensity on most days. Borg scale 5-7	Twice a week total body workout: 1-2 exercises per body part, 3 sets, 12 reps. Perform exercises slowly, rest 30-40 seconds between sets. Breathe.	Every day 20-30 minutes. Add meditation, breathing and/ or yoga.	Calorie requirement to maintain weight. Consume oily fish/ flaxseed oil and powder, green tea, plenty of fruit and whole grains.	Minimum 8 hours of deep sleep

| Weight and Fitness Maintenance | 5 times a week: twice HIIT at Borg scale 7-9; 2 longer, slower workouts, incorporating a step or dance aerobic class for variety and enjoyment. | Twice a week whole body routine: 2 exercises per body part, 4 sets of 12 reps each. | Every day 10 minutes. | Balanced diet with required calories. | 6-8 hours |

Aerobic Exercises

Aerobic, meaning 'with oxygen,' involves moderate-intensity exercise to maintain stamina and cardiovascular fitness. It enhances the cardiorespiratory system, improving heart and lung conditions. The body derives energy through three main processes, primarily from adenosine triphosphate (ATP). In Aerobic Metabolism, in low-to moderate-intensity exercise, continuous oxygen supply converts nutrients to ATP through the Krebs cycle. Sustained by slow-twitch muscle fibers, this type can last 2-3 hours, relying mainly on carbohydrates for ATP. Adequate pre-exercise nourishment, termed carb loading, is essential for long-duration activities like marathons.

Compound Exercises

Compound exercises are multi-joint moves that use several muscle groups at once. Compound exercises are very important because they can improve your overall health, physique, and strength. Apart from building muscles, compound exercises also improve bone strength, joint flexibility, and shed fat. For example, a squat uses the quadriceps, hamstrings, glutes, calves, and core muscles at the same time.

Some compound exercises and muscles they work on are mentioned in the table provided below:

Table 15.4: Compound exercises

Some compound exercises and their target muscles		
Exercise	Overview	Target Muscles
Squat	Squats are a lower body exercise that is excellent for building leg strength and overall lower body power.	Quadriceps, Glutes, Hamstrings, Calves, Core
Bench Press	The Bench Press is a fundamental upper-body exercise for building chest strength and size.	Pectoralis, Shoulders, and Triceps
Deadlifts	Deadlifts are one of the most effective full-body strength exercises.	Hamstrings, Glutes, Quadriceps, Latissimus, Trapezius, and Core
Pull-up	Pull-ups are excellent for building upper body strength.	Latissimus, Biceps, Triceps, Trapezius, Rear Delts, and Core
Lunge	Lunges are versatile lower-body exercise that helps improve balance	Quadriceps, Glutes, Hamstrings,

		and stability.	Calves, Core
Shoulder Press		Shoulder Press is a key exercise for developing shoulder strength and definition.	Shoulders, Pectoralis, Trapezius, and Triceps

What are the benefits of compound exercises?

1. **Enhanced Strength** – Compound lifts engage large muscle groups, promoting overall strength and muscle development.

2. **Time-Saving** – Incorporating compound lifts into your workout routine can save time compared to isolating individual muscles. They target multiple muscle groups simultaneously, allowing you to get more done.

3. **Elevated Heart Rate and Calorie Burn** – Since they involve multiple muscles, compound lifts can elevate your heart rate more than isolation exercises and help you burn more calories during the workout.

4. **Increased Growth Hormones** – Compound lifts stimulate the release of hormones like testosterone and growth hormones, which aid in muscle growth.

5. **Burn Fat** – As compound exercises work multiple parts of the body at the same time, it's very easy to turn up the heat and use the body's energy and endurance. It helps to develop muscle tissue.

6. **Build Muscles** – Compound exercises are imperative as they build all your muscles at once, creating a well-proportioned physique.

7. **Strengthen Joints** – At once, all the joints in your body, as well as bones, will benefit from the movements. This helps to create stronger, more durable, and more flexible joints.

8. **Better Posture** – Compound exercises promote strength, stability, and growth, so it benefits posture. A lot of compound exercises, such as squats and deadlifts, will help align muscles joints, and bones in the correct stature.

9. **Increased Strength** – Compound exercises can help build strength more than any other exercise or sport. Compound exercises demand strength from your toes, all the way to your head. This means your body will develop better strength and endurance.

10. **Better Body Balance** – Core is one of the main reasons why people prefer compound exercises over isolation exercises. Compound exercises help stabilize your whole body by developing strength and endurance in your entire body. Having a strong core is important as it helps to ease joints, prevent injury, and always maintain proper posture.

11. **Can Be Done at any Intensity** – Weightlifting can be done at any intensity that suits you best, at your own pace and level.

Compound exercises are versatile and adaptable, making them accessible for individuals of all fitness levels. The key is to make consistent progress in your fitness journey, whether you need to rest between exercises, lift little or heavy weights, or rely on your body weight.

As long as you are progressing a little bit every time, you are on the right track.

Wrapping up my book, it's crucial to present summaries of the four remaining narratives. While these stories may appear distinct initially, it's imperative not to disregard their shared theme: the importance of grasping the patient's viewpoint, stress factors, and fundamental concerns.

All stories to be put brackets.

> **Story 1: Unknown Misery in life**
>
> Myra, 24 year old Architect was perfectly fine on Sunday but met with a motorcycle accident the very next day's morning. When she opened her eyes after 4 days; she realised the whole of her right hand was cut or amputated from the shoulder. Her right hand being her dominant hand put her in a tight spot as she was the sole earner of the family and her work required her hand. When she was brought to me for rehabilitation she was in extreme pain but was very loco with self-esteem and depressed. It was not enough that one doctor can treat herfully. we jointly Rehabilitated her fully with prosthetic hand with holistic approach with the help of psychiatrist, psychologists. She was Happy at the end of treatment
>
> **Story 2: Life trauma**
>
> Special needs children could be children suffering from—., cerebral palsy, muscular disease, ADHD, AUTISM spectrum disorder, Down syndrome team approach and family support. Anaya, 8-year-old, Down syndrome child was brought to me for pain management. During the treatment, my mother told me that Anaya is not accepted by any friend and they are not invited to family or friends' social gatherings as looks are not acceptable in "normal" looking children. It is not the mental

trauma to the child but to the parents. Mother told me everywhere she was blamed for having this child.

Story 3: Stress can be a killer

In an Emergency, Abbay, a 50-year-old male was brought with a severe cardiac arrest and chest pain. Doctors advised to admit him in an ICU immediately. Looking at doctor and one hand on chest due to pain, he asked the doctor if he can send one important email otherwise his job will be at stake. He was worried about the job more than death, is real truth of this Era.

Story 4: Body shaming

Losing weight and looking good in minimal time and money coupled with a quick method without much effort is the wish of the time. Geeta, 55 years old patient was overweight and was always teased by her family, husband and friends. She succumbed to a quick fix— liposuction from a place which was not recognised & was loco in fare. She had septicemia post procedure and died immediately. Was it worth to lose life this way to look beautiful?

All people in above stories, faced different problems, but they required only one approach, a holistic one, to understand their need and not to treat only symptoms but treat them as a whole human beings.

In my practise I have seen STRESSS is a major factor which affects body and mind.

In order to have healthy life span you need to follow the healthy you routine.

The only message of this book is to "Die young in BODY and MIND as late as possible". TYBM- Train your body and mind to achieve EPS- Extra Potential Stimulation to overcome hurdles.

Combining the intrinsic power of our body and mind with EPS (extra potential stimulation), enables us to go beyond conventional boundaries and find innovative solutions to life's challenges. This book is based on these two mantras, TYBM and EPS, with the aim of empowering you to enhance your health span from childhood to adulthood.

Living to be old in good adequate health in mind and body is moreover a form of freedom. It creates an opportunity to think, to read, to love, to enjoy yourself.

Good Health and well-being are essential aspects of our lives that contribute to overall happiness and quality of life.

Life span to health span is a journey.

UNLOCK YOUR BEST SELF—***TRAIN YOUR BODY, STIMULATE YOUR MIND, AND LIVE YOUTHFUL IN BOTH, ALL THE WAY TO THE END***.

The 12 Commands: Simple Rules to live healthy life.

1. Cardio-train 20-40 minutes a day, 5 days a week.

2. Do not fear weight training but train with weights at least 2-3 times a week.

3. Stretch every day for about 10-15 minutes.

4. Do not undertake starvation diets, use gimmicks or partake in unhealthy practices.

5. Include all the food groups in thy diet.

6. Do not try to mimic thy best friend's or neighbor's fitness schedule or diet.

7. Do not follow the latest fitness trends without first checking their safety and efficacy.

8. Drink at least 8-10 glasses of water a day and restrict alcohol and sweetened beverages.

9. Have adequate rest.

10. Breathe, smile, have fun and not take thyself too seriously all the time.

11. Do stretching, strengthening and mobility exercises.

12. Keep moving, Now, Then, Always.

Concentrate on your health span rather than your life span.

BASIC STRETCHING EXERCISES

Triceps Stretch

Lateral Stretch

Groin Stretch

Quadriceps Stretch

Hamstring Stretch

Calf Stretch

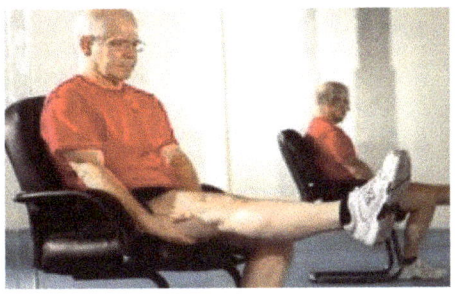

Basic level mobility exercises for beginners

Arm lifts (standing)

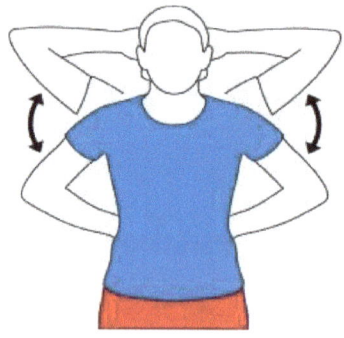

Arm stretch (standing)

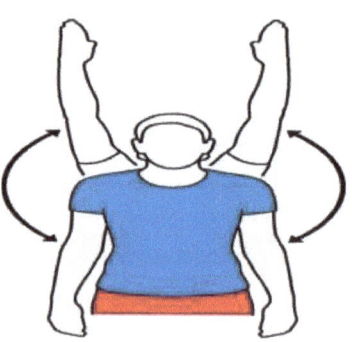

Shoulder stretch

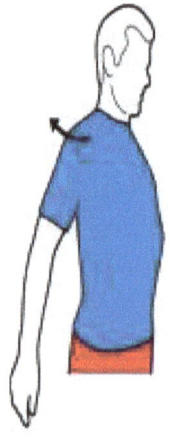

Resistance band stretch for shoulders

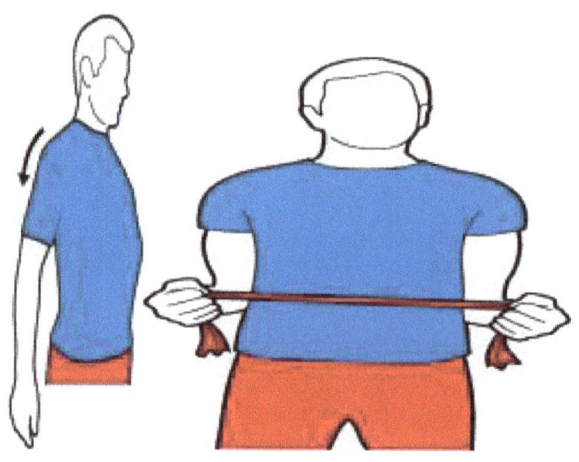

Shoulder circle

Table stretch

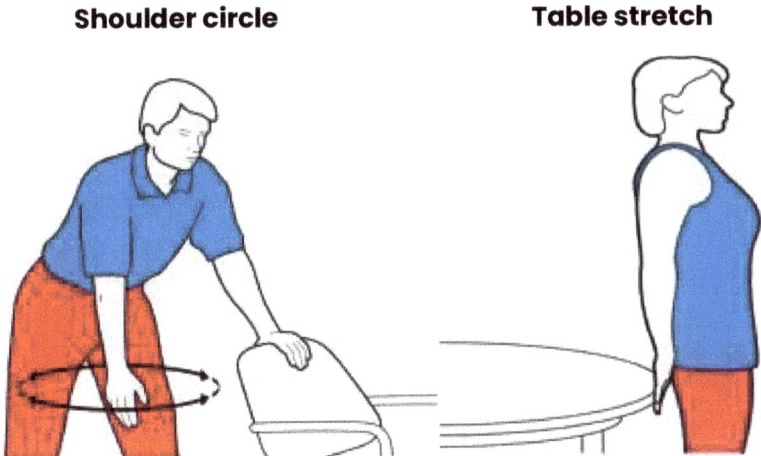

Knees to chest

Deep stomach muscle tone

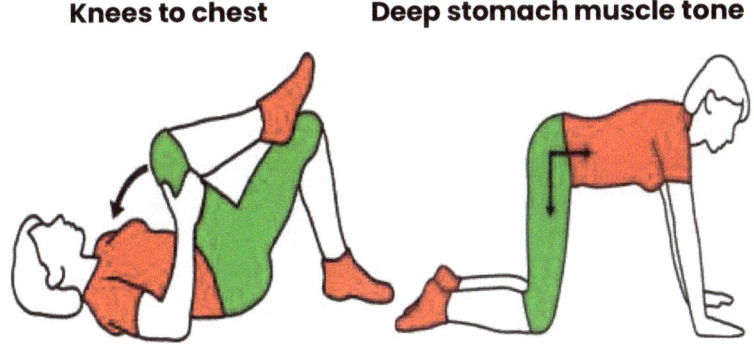

Back stabiliser

Arm raise

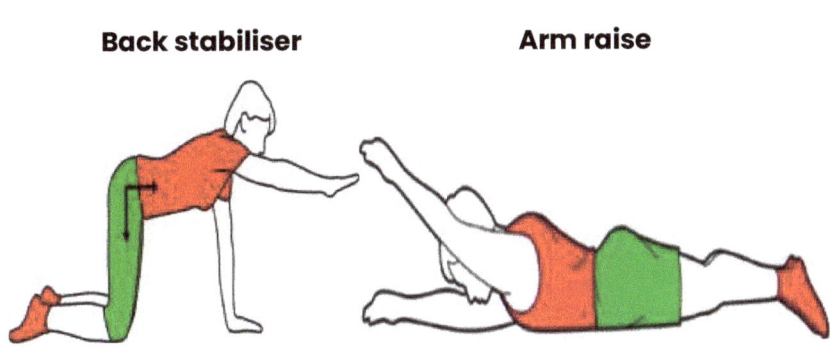

Leg raise

Deep lunge

Bridging

Hip flexion

Short arc quadriceps exercise

Knee lift

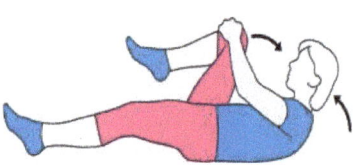

Hip extension

Hip abduction (standing)

Heel to buttock

Squats

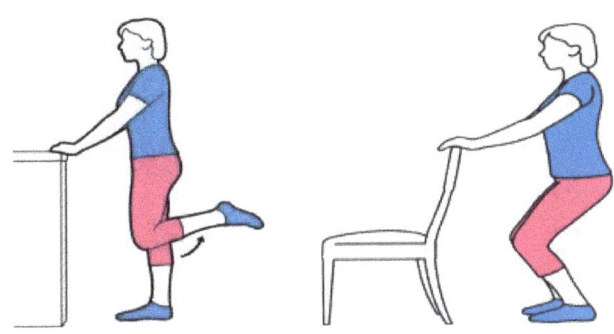

Basic one leg standing balance

Advanced balance

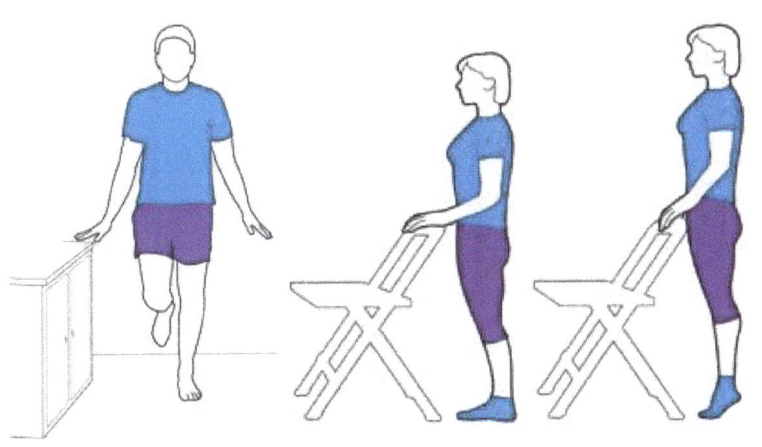

As long as you are progressing a little bit every time, you are on the right track.

Moderate-intensity aerobic/cardiorespiratory exercises

150 mins every week
at least 5 days, each time 30 mins or longer

Vigorous-intensity aerobic/cardiorespiratory exercises

75 mins every week
at least 3 days, each time 20 mins or longer

Muscle strengthening
twice a week

Stretching
2-3 times per week

Reference: The World Health Organization and the American College of Sports Medicine (ACSM)

Below are some examples of full body compound exercises (BEGINNER LEVEL):

Some examples of full body compound exercises (ADVANCED LEVEL):

Aerobic exercise: Perform at least 10 minutes continuously per day.

Strength exercise: Perform 2 to 4 sets of maximum repetitions until fatigue.

- Walking
- Running
- Jumping Jacks
- Split Squat
- Push-up
- Abdominal Crunch
- Step-up onto Chair
- Squat
- Cycling
- Up and Down Steps
- Plank
- Immersion on Chair

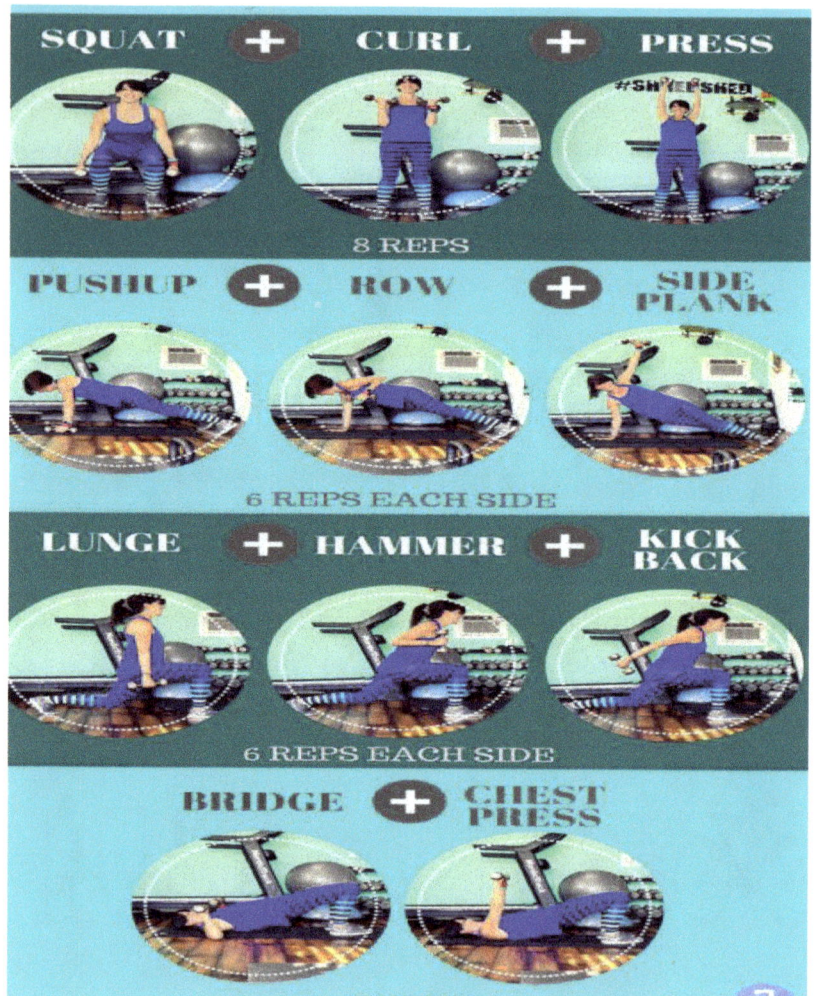

Some examples of exercises (ADVANCED LEVEL):

Difference between compound exercises VS Isolated exercises

Exercise Tracker

Maintain these sheets so that you can keep a track of your workout, spot mistakes and make progress. Maintain the tracker for 7 days in a row and it can teach you much more than any fitness guide.

Weight training days

Date	Exercise	Sets	Weights (Lbs Or Kgs)	Repetitions

Cardio Days

Date	Exercise	Speed/Rpm	Incline/Resistance	Time (Mins)	Distance (Kms)	Rpe

Acknowledgments

This Book is conceived and written from the minds and experiences of many beautiful people, patients and friends, I met during my professional and personal journey of life and from their conversations.

Everybody sees the world from their window and has their own experiences while moving in this world. But when you listen and gather the experiences of each one of them, it is like a beautiful puzzle put together and you see the world as a whole and with a non-charred beauty.

I would really thank many people in my life, but than in acknowledgements, I can only thank people whose names I know and who know that they have helped me immensely. So here goes, in order of preference.

My entire family and friends for wholeheartedly supporting every venture I undertake including the Book written, and especially my Husband Sanjiv, for being my rock for my each adventure.

My patients, who gave me the respect and love that made me achieve the meaning of my name being perceptive and melodious. . I really owe everything to my patients.

The doctors who supported me as a Team member. My Team for always covering up for me. My Teachers, professors for their patient, kind and compassionate teaching.

Finally a huge thanks to you - the Readers, who make a book, hot writers, publishes and marketers.

References:

Abbas, J., Wang, D., Su, Z., & Ziapour, A. (2021). The role of social media in the advent of COVID-19 pandemic: Crisis management, mental health challenges and implications. Risk Management and Healthcare Policy, 14, 1917.

Akbari, M., & Hossaini, S. M. (2018). The relationship of spiritual health with quality of life, mental health, and burnout: The mediating role of emotional regulation. Iran J Psychiatry, 13(1), 22–31.

Crandall, K.J & Steenbergen, K. I. (2015). Older adults' functional performance and health knowledge after a combination exercise, health education, and bingo game. Gerontology and Geriatric Medicine (1), 233372141561320.

Doyle, K. (2013, Marc 11). How to assess muscle strength in older adults. [Internet]. Minneapolis Personal Trainer and Health Coach.

2013. https://ksbodyshop.com/assess-muscle-strength-older-adults/

Grover, S., Dua, D., Sahoo, S., Mehra, A., Nehra, R., & Chakrabarti, S. (2020). Why all COVID-19 hospitals should have mental health professionals: The importance of mental health in a worldwide crisis. Asian Journal of Psychiatry, 51, 102147.

Henriksson, J. (1995). Muscle fuel selection: Effect of exercise and training. Proceedings of the Nutrition Society, 54(1), 125–138. https://doi.org/10.1079/pns19950042.

Muscular Endurance (2023, Mar 11). http://www.intrainingsports.com/fitness-blog/muscular-endurance.html.

National Institute on Aging (NIA). (2008). In Encyclopedia of global Health. SAGE Publications, Inc. http://dx.doi.org/10.4135/9781412963855.n838.

The Borg rating of perceived exertion (RPE) scale. (2016). In Care of the obese in advanced practice nursing. Springer Publishing Company. http://dx.doi.org/10.1891/9780826123589.ap15

Vigelsø, A., Gram, M., Wiuff, C., Andersen, J., Helge, J., & Dela, F. (2015). Six weeksâ€TM aerobic retraining after two weeksâ€TM immobilization restores leg lean mass and aerobic capacity but does not fully rehabilitate leg strength in young and older men. Journal of Rehabilitation Medicine, 47(6), 552–560. https://doi.org/10.2340/16501977-1961.

Appendix I

THE ASIAN RECOMMENDATION FOR BMI BY THE WHO

BMI	
<16	Severely underweight
16.0–16.9	Moderately underweight
17.0–18.49	Mildly underweight
18.5–24.9	Normal range
> 25	Overweight
25–29.9	Preobese
>30	Obese
30–34.9	Obese class 1
35–39.9	Obese class 2
>40	Obese class 3

Source: WHO Expert Consultation, 'Appropriate Body-Mass Index for Asian Populations and Its Implications for Policy and Intervention Strategies', The Lancet, 363 (2004).

Appendix II

MEASURING INTENSITY USING THE RESTING HEART RATE

This method for figuring intensity takes individual differences into consideration. Here is one of them:

1. Subtract age from 220 to find maximum heart rate (MHR).

2. Subtract resting heart rate (see below) from maximum heart rate to determine heart rate reserve (HRR).

3. Take 70 per cent of heart rate reserve to determine heart rate raise.

4. Add heart rate raise to resting heart rate to find target heart rate.

For example, a 70 percent intensity for a 30-year-old is calculated as follows:

220−30=190 (MHR)

If resting heart rate (RHR) is 70 bpm, then 190−70 = 120 (HRR)

70 percent of HRR = 84 bpm heart rate raise

Target heart rate = heart rate raise + RHR= 84+70 =154 bpm

Appendix III

HOW DO YOU EVALUATE HOW MANY CALORIES YOU BURN WHILE WORKING OUT?

If you don't have the MET denoted on your cardio machine, or if you are not using a machine, how do you calculate the number of calories you are expending from physical activity? Simply multiply your body weight in kilograms by the MET value (which is noted in the chart below) and the duration of the activity (in hours: take the number of minutes you exercise and divide by 60).

For example, you weigh 60 kg and you bike at a value of 4 MET for 40 minutes, you have expended the following number of calories:

4 (MET) x 60 (kg) x (40/60) (hours) = 160 calories

MET VALUES FOR SPECIFIC ACTIVITIES		
Type of Activity	**Description**	**METS**
Bicycling	10 mph-leisurely paces	4
	10-11.9 mph	6
	12-13.9 mph	8
Aerobics	Low impact, low intensity	5
	High intensity	7
	Step 15-20 cm	8.5
	Jazzercise	6

	Ski machine	7
	Stair master	9
	Water aerobics	4
Running	Jog/walk combination (jogging combination of less than 10 min)	6
	Jogging 5 mph	9
	Jogging 6 mph	10
	Jogging 6.7 mph	11
	Jogging 7 mph	11.5
	Jogging 7.5 mph	12.5
	Jogging 8 mph	13.5
	Jogging 8.6 mph	14
	Jogging 9 mph	15
	Jogging 10 mph	16
Badminton	Social	4.5
	Competitive	7
Basketball	Social	6
	Competitive	8
Football	Competitive	9

Other games	Golf	4.5
	Golf, carrying the clubs	5.5
	Hockey	8
	Horseback riding	4
	Rugby	10
	Rock climbing, ascending rock	11
	Rope jumping fast	12
	Rope jumping-moderate	10
	Rope jumping-slow	8
	Soccer	10
	Squash	12
	Table tennis	4
	Tai chi	4
	Tennis general	7
	Tennis singles	8
	Track and field (shot-put, discus, hammer throw)	4
	Track and field (high jump, long jump, javelin, pole	6

	vault)	
	Track and field (steeplechase, hurdles)	10
	Backpacking	7
Walking	Less than 2 mph-level ground	2
	3 mph-level ground	3.3
	3.5-level ground	3.8
	4 mph-level ground	5
	4.5 mph-level ground	6.3
	3.5 mph-uphill	6
Swimming	Freestyle: fast, vigorous effort	10
	Freestyle: slow to moderate pace	7
	Backstroke	7
	Breaststroke, general	10
	Butterfly, general	11

Source: Ainsworth, B. E. et al, 'Compendium of Physical Activities: An Update of Activity Codes and MET Intensities', Medicine and Science in Sport and Exercise (2000), $499.

Appendix IV

Rating of perceived exertion: Borg scale

6	No exertion at all	No muscle fatigue, breathlessness or difficulty in breathing.
7	Extremely light	Very, very light.
8		
9	Very light	Like walking slowly for a short while. Very easy to talk.
10		
11	Light	Like a light exercise at your own pace.
12	Moderate	
13	Somewhat hard	Fairly strenuous and breathless. Not so easy to talk.
14		
15	Hard	Heavy and strenuous. An upper limit for fitness training, as when running or walking fast.
16		
17	Very hard	Very strenuous. You are very tired and breathless. Very difficult to talk.
18		
19	Extremely hard	The most strenuous effort you have ever experienced.

| 20 | Maximal exertion | Maximal heaviness. |

SOURCE: Borg RPE Scale®
Ratings (R) of Perceived (P) Exertion (E).
© Gunnar Borg, 1970, 1998, 2017
English

www.ingramcontent.com/pod-product-compliance
Lightning Source LLC
LaVergne TN
LVHW072334080526
838199LV00108B/381